Fearfully and Wonderfully Made:
My Christian Journey with ADHD

Fearfully and Wonderfully Made:
My Christian Journey with ADHD

By
David Michael Carrillo

gentlewind
MUSIC MINISTRY
A Publication Of
GentleWind Music Ministry
Indianapolis, IN

A publication of
GentleWind Music Ministry
P.O. Box 44601
Indianapolis, IN 46244
(317) 767-4215
www.gentlewindmusic.com

ISBN 978-1-4303-0963-5
© 2006 by David Michael Carrillo/GentleWind Music Ministry
All rights reserved
Printed in the United States of America
Published October 2006
First Edition

Photography provided by David Michael Carrillo,
GentleWind Music Ministry, and Laurie Vandiford Hobbs.

Song lyrics to Faithful, He Flew Away, Wounds and Pain, Fearfully and Wonderfully Made excerpted from *A Pilgrim's Progress: The Best of GentleWind Music*, released March 2005, by David Michael Carrillo. Song lyrics to Trust In You excerpted from *I Surrender: The Early Years*, released February 2003, by David Michael Carrillo. Song lyrics to House of Mirrors written by David Michael Carrillo, The Songs of GentleWind © 2006 (Ascap), administered by GentleWind Music Ministry.

Song lyrics to Honeytree and Diamond in the Rough excerpted from *The Way I Feel* (1974, Word Music) and *Melodies in Me* (1978, Word Music), by Nancy Honeytree.

Scripture quotations are taken from the New International Version © 1973, 1978, 1984, by the International Bible Society.

Book design/layout, and editorial assistance
Kathryn Patricia McDermott

Cover design/layout, and editorial assistance
Laurie Vandiford Hobbs

Dedication

I dedicate this book to all who feel helpless living with ADHD. May you find hope and healing from the journey of one pilgrim who has rediscovered God's profound love and purposes in the midst of deep wounds and pain. This book is also for Ryan Zachariah Noll, my brother in the faith, who shares my journey.

Acknowledgments

I must thank those who contributed to the development of this book.

My Parents, Mike & Mary Carrillo:
For the love and support you have shown me throughout my life. For believing in me even when I had lost faith. To my father, whose quiet faith spoke louder through his actions than through his words. To my mom, who has been the best prayer warrior a son could have.

My sister, Stephanie Carrillo-Hays:
Wow, Stephanie, all those years of my getting on your nerves pays off now in a book. Joking aside, thank you for the love and support you have shown me throughout the years. I am glad the experience of living with me turned out to be a positive influence on your work as a school teacher, especially as you help other students who have ADHD. The world needs more teachers like you.

Nancy Honeytree:
Your ministry, music, and love for Jesus Christ have had a deep impact on me since I was a teenager. What an honor it has been to know you as a co-laborer and friend for the Gospel and to serve on your ministry board. I also want to say thank you for fulfilling a long-time dream by doing two concerts with me in Sheboygan, WI.

Anthony Todd Ping & Ryan Zachariah Noll:
You guys are more like my younger brothers than friends. How can I thank you enough for putting up with my "colorful moments?" Todd, thank you for helping me to open up and step outside the lines. Zachariah, thank you for helping me to see the world through the eyes of love and respect.

Sherrie Connell & Angela Connell:
You both gave me the inspiration to start talking about my ADHD and to offer workshops for teachers and parents. Thank you for the wonderful years of friendship, home-cooked meals, and Southern hospitality.

Katie McDermott:
If not for you, this book would still be drifting in my mind. How can I ever thank you for stepping in and helping me put into words what has been in my heart for so long? I appreciate the long hours you endured listening to hours upon hours of my ramblings on tape. Somehow you managed to turn all that rambling into a book!

As he went along, he saw a man blind from birth.

His disciples asked him,

"Rabbi, who sinned, this man or his parents,

that he was born blind?"

"Neither this man nor his parents sinned,"

said Jesus, "but this happened so that

the work of God might be displayed in his life."

John 9:1-3

For you created my inmost being;

you knit me together in my mother's womb.

I praise you because I am fearfully and wonderfully made;

your works are wonderful....

Psalm 139:13-14

Table of Contents

Chapter 1, Was I A Mistake? 1

Chapter 2, The Learning Show 13

Chapter 3, Ties That Bind 23

Chapter 4, The Caged Bird Sings 35

Chapter 5, Betrayal 45

Chapter 6, The Prodigal Son 53

Chapter 7, Searching For Home 59

Chapter 8, Learning To Trust 67

Chapter 9, Fearfully And Wonderfully Made 79

Chapter 10, Living A Colorful Life 85

Lyrics to *Fearfully and Wonderfully Made* 91

CHAPTER 1
Was I A Mistake?

Out of the depths I cry to you, O Lord;
O Lord, hear my voice.
Psalm 130:1-2

"Something's wrong with your son; he won't tell us."

My teacher wrote these words on a piece of paper and pinned it to my shirt for my mother to read when I got home. It was 1971, the first day of kindergarten, and I was five years old.

As it turned out this was not to be an uncommon event. Throughout kindergarten the end of the school day was marked for me not by a bell, but by the slight tug of my collar as my teacher hastily decorated my shirt with a safety pin and a slip of paper.

I was reprimanded for a variety of reasons – most of which involved not sitting still, or talking too loudly, or distracting my classmates – and by the time class was over, my misdeeds were branded to my clothing like a huge scarlet letter. When I boarded the school bus, the driver required me sit next to one of the "good" students, that is, one of the students who knew how to behave. That student's job was to make sure that I behaved, too, or that at least I remained sufficiently contained until the time we reached my stop.

On this particular day in 1971, however, I did not get a note pinned to my shirt because I was too talkative or fidgety. It was the first day of kindergarten, and I had to use the bathroom.

The bathroom in my class was like no bathroom I had seen before. It had a small white sink and a small white toilet – all child sized. Most kids would probably consider that to be cool, but to me the miniature bathroom was neither cool nor normal. In fact, it looked freakishly small, completely *ab*normal.

The classroom also had small tables and small chairs, but for some reason that didn't bother me. Maybe it was because I had never been in a kindergarten classroom before and, as a result, I had no point of reference. The bathroom, however, bothered me, and nothing could ease my anxiety about it. My fear was that if I tried to go, I might miss the toilet. So in my mind there was only one solution: I refused to go to the bathroom the whole day.

My teacher never knew this was the problem, but sensed I was stressed about something. She asked me all day what was wrong. I didn't tell her. I *couldn't* tell her – not because I was embarrassed, but because I literally could not find the words to describe why I was upset. Unfortunately, my inability to verbalize my thoughts and feelings was a constant and frustrating struggle for me.

As a child I could never explain to people what I felt inside. I didn't understand the names of the emotions. Anger, fear, sadness, joy – these were abstract concepts that carried no meaning for me. My emotions were like shadow puppets dancing madly on a wall. They were animated and often wreaked havoc, but I could not mentally grasp them or label them in terms that made sense to me. I bottled up my feelings because I simply did not know the words to describe them.

And so, on this day, I went home with a note that said, "Something's wrong....he won't tell us."

* * * * *

As is the case for most children with attention deficit hyperactivity disorder (ADHD), I was in kindergarten when I first sensed I was different from other children my age. I remember not being able to socialize with my peers, not feeling connected to them. I was quiet and self-focused when my classmates were playing. I wanted to talk or play when they were working. We never seemed to be in sync. I can think of many examples.

Do you remember those stop-drop-and-roll bomb drills in elementary school? Well, probably only some of you do. Keep in mind we were still in the Cold War during the early 70s and constantly bracing for a communist country like the Soviet Union or Cuba to attack the United States. Stop-drop-and-roll was a practice run to prepare you to safely and quickly find cover in the event of a sudden bomb attack on school grounds. It was similar to what most of you might experience during a tornado drill. When you heard the alarm, usually a long, piercing whistle or buzzing sound, you were required to stop what you were doing, drop to the floor, and roll under your desk or the closest protective cover.

One day I remember sitting at a desk in my classroom with headphones on, listening to a recording, totally oblivious to the drill when it started. My attention was focused intently on the music. I never heard the alarm, yet was instantly startled by the fast-approaching click-click-click of my teacher's high-heeled shoes.

Repetitive sounds like that have always attracted me. To this day, I can be distracted easily by a distinctive, rhythmic sound and become lost in it. This odd attraction applies equally to rounded shapes and repetitive, circular motions.

David Michael Carrillo

Television, for example, fascinated me as a child – not just the images, but the box itself and the way it enclosed the rounded shape of the screen. It didn't matter to me if the set was turned on or off. In fact, my parents recall that on several Halloween nights while trick-or-treating, I would bypass the candy bowl and run straight into our neighbors' houses in order to check out the shapes of their TV sets.

Movie theater screens were exciting, too, but watching the curtains open and close – wow, that was the best entertainment. I was known to throw a royal five-year-old fit if somebody were to sit in front of me blocking the screen, or if I missed the opening of the curtains before the movie began. At home, I opened and closed the curtains in my living room until the constant swishing noise drove my mother to the brink of insanity.

At school, I loved to follow the sweeping motion of the projection screens as the teachers pulled them down and pushed them back up again. And watching ribbons of film wind around the reel of a 35mm film projector was more of a treat than the subject of the film itself. But record players, especially spinning turntables, were like eye candy. What really captivated me was the way the music seemed to be in sync with the turntable rhythm.

A gift that I wanted more than anything else as a child was a portable close-and-play phonograph by Kenner. It was a little record player you could take anywhere. It ran on batteries and played 45s. My mother thought it was a strange thing for a child my age to want, and casually dismissed it at the time. But one year soon after, my parents gave me a music-box television set, which became one of my most treasured childhood possessions. I guess it's no surprise that listening to and creating music remains one of my favorite activities.

As the bomb drill went into full swing around me, it was the rapid click-click-click of my teacher's heels that pulled my attention away from the music recording. I looked up and saw people running and ducking under their desks.

My teacher yelled at me to get under the desk, and then she rushed to the windows to close all the curtains. I sat frozen in my chair, dazed by the mayhem. I had no idea what was happening. I understood only that I was being reprimanded – again.

That whole episode was kind of a metaphor for my childhood years. I was forever lost in my own world, hopelessly out of touch with the rest of the world, and quickly absorbing, although not always comprehending, the feelings of rejection and anxiety that were steadily seeping into my mind.

* * * * *

My kindergarten teacher determined that something was *wrong* with me, and that summer the school tested me. As far as I know, the expression "ADHD" did not exist then (in fact, I don't remember hearing it until the mid-1990s); another more nebulous one did: minimal brain dysfunction. My IQ and comprehension levels were low. I was behind my peers academically. And socially, I acted more like a three-year-old than a six-year-old.

I was also dyslexic and didn't need a test to confirm it. Reading was always a challenge for me. I was raised in a church called First Assembly of God in Whittier, CA, and I remember that when I looked at the words on the marquee, I saw "God's First Assembly." Every time my parents tried to correct me I contradicted them because I was convinced I saw the words exactly as I said them.

And math? I simply did not comprehend it. Numbers were foreign to me. They were interesting shapes, nothing more. In school, the highest level of math I learned was how to divide whole numbers. I never learned fractions, geometry, or algebra. But strangely enough, if I were to see an every-day application of a mathematical principle, *then* I would get it. Percentages I never fathomed on paper, but when I was taught that 10 percent of my earnings should go to God, *tithing*, then I started to understand. Later as a teenager, when I worked the cash registers at McDonald's and at a Christian bookstore, math finally started to make sense.

Learning, I would discover, was a completely visual experience for me. If you did not paint pictures in my mind while telling a story, or engage me in a subject in a dramatic, 3D kind of way, then I was lost. On the other hand, if the subject was something that I really, *really* wanted to learn, then I could apply 150 percent of my mental energy to it. It was a strange phenomenon. I guess you might call it selective concentration.

What was the verdict after the series of tests conducted on me that summer after kindergarten? I was classified as behaviorally and "educably handicapped" (EH) and placed in the school's EH class for the first grade. Twelve other students, mostly boys, were my classmates. Most of them took some kind of medication; a few of them were bullies; none of them became my friend. I would stay in that class for five years.

* * * * *

The self-contained, special education classroom was probably a kind of pioneering project at that time. The goal was to help us overcome our educational handicaps so that we could be mainstreamed into a regular classroom.

But I really don't remember doing much of anything in that class that could be considered educational. Without knowing the exact source or nature of our individual "dysfunctions," the teachers, I think, had neither the resources nor the training to work with us effectively. There was no homework. We did not learn any study habits. In fact, I did not even learn to read.

The actual goals in the classroom were much different. One goal, for example, was to stay in our chair, and another was not to make noise, both of which I failed to master, of course, because the two things that I really could not do were to sit still and to be quiet.

My peers in the EH class spent most of their free time on the playground and in the hallways trying desperately to prove they were not weird, that they were not outcasts. They often started fist fights to command some semblance of respect from the regular kids who knew us only as the "special" students.

I was an easy target for the bullies. The school administrators had the mentality that "boys will be boys." If you got picked on, you should defend yourself – that seemed to be a boyhood law of nature. But my mother always taught me not to fight back, so I became a punching bag on the playground and a receptacle for verbal harassments and name-calling in the hallways.

One day during a recess period, one of the boys in my EH class jumped on my back and knocked the breath out of me. I was terrified because I could not breathe; I had never felt so panic-stricken. None of the teachers on the playground realized my distress or came to help me. When the bell rang to go back to class, everyone left. I was alone and horrified, but eventually calmed down to the point that I could take a few breaths. When I returned to class I was punished for tardiness.

I had no friends in school. I envied all of the kids around me. The normal ones I envied because they were "normal," which made me feel inadequate. The bullies I envied because even though they got into trouble, people respected them, feared them, even liked them sometimes. Nobody regarded me in any of those ways.

I began to withdraw emotionally, socially, and physically. Although I was a ball of energy at home, at school I became increasingly more quiet and reclusive. Brick by brick, I started to build around my heart that wall of defense that kids who face rejection on a daily basis so desperately retreat to as a safe shelter.

*****

One day in the spring of 1972 my teacher took me out for a special teacher-student outing. This was something she liked to do with each student. It was a rare occasion to have your teacher's undivided attention, much less to share time together that was meant to be just plain fun, so this trip was something I really looked forward to.

My teacher and I went to the library and then to the car wash; that was all, nothing extraordinary. But to me it was a treat, and precious time well spent. I felt truly *special* that afternoon – in the very best sense of the word.

At the end of our outing my teacher drove me home and asked me to wait in the car. After a few minutes, she came back to the car and told me to go inside. When I went through the door, I found my mother in tears, and my father comforting her. I was dumbfounded. I hesitantly asked what was wrong, confused by the complete break in the mood of the day.

My mother said, "Your teacher says you never smile, David Michael. You're always sad." Now today my face naturally carries a smile, and people would be surprised to see me without one, but back then people outside of my family often said I looked sad. And on this day, even my teacher had been unable to see beyond my (apparent) sullen facial expression to detect the genuine happiness I had felt during our time together.

Soon after that brief visit with my teacher, my parents took me to see a psychiatrist. Every Monday night, my dad drove me to Los Angeles to visit with a woman whom I remember most for the yellow, three-story, wooden doll house that sat in the corner of her office.

Toy cars and trucks never interested me as a child, but something captivated me about doll houses. Whenever we went to the psychiatrist's office I would go straight to the doll house and try to straighten it up. It always looked messy to me, and I felt compelled to set up the rooms and rearrange the furniture. It was one of the first memories I have of my emerging "neat freak" tendencies, although it would be awhile before I would tidy up my own room as meticulously as I arranged all the rooms in that doll house.

After several sessions, the psychiatrist and my parents decided to put me on medication, Ritalin, I think. I remember only a container of little white pills and the fact that when I took one, it either knocked me out or reduced me to a sleepy, agitated state.

One time while I was on the medication I recall going to the doctor for an exam. Whether my perception was true or muddied by the effects of the medication I'm not certain, but the doctor seemed extremely gruff. He wanted to check my throat and ordered me to open my mouth: "Wider. Wider!" I could not seem to open my mouth wide enough to allow him to get the tongue depressor all the way inside. I started to gag on the stick, so he pressed me down on the table and barked at me to open my mouth wider.

This small trauma helped to launch one of my greatest childhood fears. As the doctor yelled at me to open my mouth wider, I envisioned my throat shrinking and was convinced that in seconds I would be gasping for air.

After that, dinner time became an ordeal for my parents – and for me. I took tiny bites of food and chewed obsessively until I was certain my food was small enough to pass down my throat. And swallowing pills? No chance - that quickly went out the window. I was taken off the little white pills. I continued to obsess about my incredible shrinking throat, and subsequently lost a lot of weight. Only my insecurities seemed to grow.

*****

There comes a point when the perpetual anxiety that some ADHD children experience slowly but surely mutates into anger, even rage. One afternoon when I was home alone, I became infuriated about something – what, I no longer remember – but I will never forget the blazing anger that consumed me. I became hysterical. I felt like I was falling apart. Standing in the center of my living room, I confronted God and screamed, "Why did you make me this way?"

Why couldn't I get along with people? Why didn't I have friends? Why was I so slow to comprehend things? Did the Lord deliberately punish me? Was he playing a trick?

I started to believe that God made a mistake; *I was a mistake*. I wondered how he could possibly choose to make me like he did. I felt like processed meat – a mysterious amalgam of leftovers, separated from the prime cuts tenderly held in reserve for a more special use. God, in his desire not to waste anything, made me from scraps. What useful purpose could I possibly serve? Overwhelmed by the agony of this new revelation, I dropped to the floor, exhausted and dejected.

She got the news that her son
Would not be like everyone
He would have challenges
And four little letters will define him
He's forced to stand on the playground
The other kids don't want him around
Mama, why was I born
To live a life of shame and scorn?

From the song *Fearfully and Wonderfully Made*
(David Michael Carrillo © 2002 The Songs of GentleWind)

David Michael Carrillo

CHAPTER 2
The Learning Show

*Be my rock of refuge, to which I can always go;
give the command to save me,
for you are my rock and my fortress.*
Psalm 71:3

After surrendering to the notion that I was a flawed byproduct of God's creative powers, I moved mechanically through life like a windmill in the fog. I wished I could have slipped away like Sleeping Beauty, rescued by a deep sleep at the age of five and allowed to slumber peacefully until my late twenties. But fate was not that kind. I had to search for other forms of escape. Television became an important one.

My fascination with the shapes of television sets gradually evolved into a hunger to consume every bit of television programming I could feast my eyes on. I liked to watch *Sesame Street*, *Fran and Ollie*, and *Mr. Rogers*, but I also liked my mother's soap operas. All of these programs appealed to me for one reason or another. But mostly, they provided a way for me to cope with the personal dramas of my life.

As Shakespeare once said, "All the world's a stage, and all the people merry players." It was much easier for me to grasp my world as a stage, a soap opera, a TV show. Fantasy was less painful than reality, but as it turned out, fantasy would also provide a way for me to learn about real life. When I was six years old, I became the lead character of my own program, *The Learning Show*.

* * * * *

The *Learning Show* actually had two dimensions to it. During school hours, the *Learning Show* was a soap opera. I was the star actor portraying the maligned, helpless victim. In real life, that wasn't hard for me. I always felt rejected, alone, insecure. Nothing in my school life was stable. The story lines were always changing. There were always tortuous twists and turns, surprise endings. People would come and go. I would simply respond by saying to myself, "Today, the character of so-and-so is now being played by so-and-so."

But outside of school, in the mornings, afternoons, and on the weekends, the *Learning Show* was a kid's show, a puppet show, and I was the host. My bedroom was the set, and my bookcase was the puppet theater. I imagined three cameras in each corner of my room, and an audience full of kids.

My puppets, the alligator and the dog, would talk with the kids about all kinds of things, or they would just do goofy things for laughs. If I got tired and wanted to watch cartoons for real, I would just say, "Hey kids, it's cartoon time!" – kind of like you would see on the *Mickey Mouse Club*, where a big screen would come up to present the cartoon feature of the day. That's how I justified watching cartoons. My audience wanted to watch them, so I watched them, too.

My mother must have thought I was crazy. I spent the first six to eight years of my life in my bedroom talking with puppets. I took them everywhere. My alligator puppet was my favorite. On Christmas Day 2005, he turned 33 years old. He's been around for as many years as I've been a Christian. He's well preserved for such an old guy. I take him out of storage once in awhile just for fun.

For many years, Alligator was my imaginary friend. He was a true friend when I had no friends. Through him I learned to do all kinds of fun voices and characters, which, ironically, later in life, helped me to get my first job out of high school as a professional puppeteer in Whittier, CA, for a kids show called the *Rainbow Mountaineers.*

For four years, I worked hard on that show and had lots of fun. I never could have imagined that it would eventually lead me to another show called *Religion in the News*, where I served as co-host and sometimes a fill-in host, covering the Christian aspects of the Indianapolis community on our CBS affiliate station.

I remember sitting in the host's chair during one of the first episodes of *Religion in the News*, looking into the camera, and thinking to myself how amazing it was that an imaginary puppet show and soap opera had led to this. Through *The Learning Show*, God in his infinite wisdom was using a little boy's imagination to help him cope with painful childhood realities, but He was also using it to prepare him for his real-life adventures as an adult.

*****

Approaching my life as if I were a character on *The Learning Show* somehow emboldened me. Instead of shutting myself out of a painful world, I was able to open myself up to people and events that, while I didn't recognize it at the time, would positively shape the course of my life in so many ways.

I remember one rainy day at school when my special education teacher asked our class to draw a picture of what we saw ourselves doing as grown-ups. I drew myself singing with a microphone in front of people, which I admit was a strange thing for me to do.

I never had voice lessons or any musical training. My only exposure to music was on those rare occasions in my EH class when, as a reward for good behavior, my teacher permitted me to listen to records with headphones. Yet, whenever my teacher gave this assignment, which for some reason she did often, I drew the same picture of myself standing on stage and singing to an audience.

My teacher was amused by my career choice but also puzzled. This was the only scene I would ever draw for this assignment. She often pressed me to draw something else, something more practical, but I stubbornly refused. This was the picture that always came to mind when I imagined myself grown up. And like my persevering soap opera character on *The Learning Show*, I wasn't about to compromise my dream – no matter how far fetched it might seem. Little did I know that in two short years I would discover with crystal clarity how that dream was destined to play out in my life.

* * * * *

At the same time that I was sketching impractical dreams at school, my parents were experiencing serious troubles in their marriage.

To this day I wonder if my parents' marriage was stressed by my ADHD and all the challenges that went with it. It is not unusual for kids to blame themselves when their parents fight, or when marriages break up, but by the age of six I was already keenly aware of how disruptive I was compared to my younger sister, and how much I seemed to test my mother's patience in particular.

Back then, I was convinced my parents' marriage was on the rocks because of me. Today, looking back, I can see that in actuality my ADHD led my family into a relationship with the Lord, which ultimately saved my parents' marriage and charted the course for my ministry.

In my EH class there was a girl whose mother, a devout Christian woman, became good friends with my mother through PTA conferences and other school events. When my mother confided to her one day that her marriage was in trouble, she invited my mother to her church, First Family Church, in Whittier, California.

My mother recalls that by God's grace she was saved the day she attended church with this kind woman. On that day, she made a commitment to the Lord to save her marriage. With His help, and with much perseverance, she – well, I should say *they* (both of my parents) – eventually succeeded. My parents celebrated their 40th wedding anniversary in January 2005.

After my mother found the Lord, she prayed for us every day. I remember many times waking up to hear the sound of her voice in the kitchen as she was praying and singing to the Lord.

Now, most mornings when I tumbled out of bed my brain instantly jumped into overdrive, but on those special mornings I found myself unusually calmed by my mother's voice. I would tip-toe to the kitchen, pry open the door, and secretly listen to her pray in song. She looked and sounded truly at peace. It wasn't a fantasy. It wasn't a scene from *The Learning Show*. It was real, and I was hungry for more.

* * * * *

My mom started taking me to church with her at First Family. That marked the formation of an incredible spiritual bond between my mother and me, one that continues to sustain our relationship today. Several weeks after our first visit to the church, I was saved, at the age of six.

Even though I was so young I remember vividly the moment I began my walk with the Lord. It was Easter 1972, and I was in Sunday school class listening to the story of the Passover. My teacher related this story very descriptively.

God told Moses to tell his people to take the blood of the lamb and to pour it on the doorframe of their houses because God was going to execute his last plague, which would be the death of every firstborn in Egypt, those in royalty and those in poverty, as well as the firstborn of all the animals.

If God saw the blood of the lamb on the door of the house, then he would pass over that house (thus the term *Passover*), and all would be blessed with the love and mercy of His protection. But if the house did not have the blood applied over the doorframe, then that house would come under God's judgment, which would result in the death of the firstborn.

To illustrate the story of the Passover, my teacher made a shadow box. It was a shoebox with a hole cut into one side. Inside the box were cutout figures of Moses, a family, and a doorframe marked with the blood of the lamb.

Now, I was a visual learner, so this exercise really grabbed my attention. Our class took turns peering inside the shadow box to see the scene of Moses and the Passover. As I took my turn and peeked into the hole, I heard my teacher say, "Children, like the marking of the lamb's blood over the door, we need the blood of the Lamb of God over our heart's door, for without the blood of Jesus Christ applied to our heart's door, we come under that same judgment as the Egyptians –

and that is death. The wages of sin are death, but the gift of God is eternal life through Christ Jesus."

As I saw the Passover scene displayed in colorful 3D images and heard my teacher's words, three thoughts came to mind.

First, I began to wonder. "My heart doesn't have that. The blood of Jesus isn't in my heart."

Second, I started to panic. "Hey, I'm also the firstborn in my family." Because I took things literally I thought to myself, "Oh my God, I'm going to die."

Finally, I determined – and this hit me hard – "I want to have the blood of Jesus on my heart's door!" Right there the Holy Spirit, through my teacher's words and the 3D images, touched me. Everything rang true. It all clicked. I held the conviction that without the Lord in my life, I would be lost.

For a small boy of six that's probably an unusual revelation, but that's how it was for me. I felt deeply that something was wrong, that there was a void in my heart, and that somehow all of that needed to change.

After class when the other kids went to the church service, I stayed behind. I had to ask my teacher, "How do I get Jesus in my life? How do I get His blood on my heart's door?"

So we sat down on miniature tables, and she told me about who Jesus was and what he did and how he wanted to be our best friend. Right there I opened my heart to the Lord. After our talk, I rushed to my mother to tell her that I had become a Christian and that Jesus was my best friend.

For many years, I had a great imaginary friend in Alligator from the *The Learning Show*, but the moment I was saved I gained a new best friend for life, and the innocence of that moment remains with me today.

Jesus is my best friend. I still talk with Him like I did as a child. He has never been to me a distant God out in the cosmos, only a friend. As I have grown in my faith, I have learned to respect Him as Lord of lords, King of kings, Creator of heaven and earth. I acknowledge his lordship, but I have never lost that child-like intimacy I felt, and still feel, since I began walking with him that Easter Sunday in 1972.

* * * * *

Two years after I was saved I received God's call into the ministry. One night my mother and I went to a revival service where I discovered an extraordinary evangelical minister named Jeff Steinberg. He leads a ministry called Masterpiece in Progress, which remains active today and is headquartered in Orlando, Florida.

I remember Mr. Steinberg as a powerful preacher. The night of the revival he sang with great conviction and joy for the Lord. But at eight years old, I was temporarily fixated on something else.

Mr. Steinberg had physical handicaps. He was missing both arms, and his legs were badly deformed. He was incredibly, I thought, the same height as me. I watched him intently. He had physical challenges; I had challenges, too. Yet, here he was on stage grasping a microphone with a hook-shaped prosthetic arm and empowering the audience with his words and song.

In a moment, I knew my true calling. I turned to my mother and said, "That's what I'm going to do someday. When I grow up, I'm going to sing and preach about Jesus just like Jeff Steinberg."

From that day forward, I can't begin to tell you how many people tried to talk me out of my dream. But I held on – past the many painful experiences to come at school, past heartbreaking trials with family and friends, past my own self doubts.

Somehow I knew deep within that God was calling me to the ministry. He picked that vocation *for me*. God planted the seed within my heart at an early age, and He knew that in its proper time it would grow to flourish into what it has become today.

There would still be many obstacles and crossroads ahead. But my means of coping with them changed dramatically. God's love for me replaced the comfortable but worn out story lines of *The Learning Show*.

I praise God that I found Him when I did. Even though I would argue with Him, run from Him, mistrust His motives (as I confess I am still inclined to do today), I have never questioned His love for me. And that has made all the difference in my life.

His name was spoken unlike before
Said he was chosen beloved of the Lord
In his heart's garden the weeds were removed
A new seed was planted and bore fruit
In the maze of his mind the light of truth shines
Dispelling the darkness of the house of mirrors

From the song *House of Mirrors*
(David Michael Carrillo © 2005 The Songs of GentleWind)

David Michael Carrillo

CHAPTER 3
Ties That Bind

*Praise be to the Lord, to God our Savior,
who daily bears our burdens.*
Psalm 68:19

Even before I was born my parents knew hardship. I say that somewhat tongue in cheek, but it was true. Both of my parents came from large families with very little money, and both of them were raised by abusive alcoholics.

My parents were still teenagers when they married. They had never been given the opportunity to observe a healthy marriage, much less the dynamics of a healthy family. But they were united in a common desire to break free from the fractured molds they came from and achieve something better together.

My mom was only 18 when she gave birth to me. She and my dad had been married 11 months. Three and a half years later, my sister was born, and the young Carrillo family began their journey together toward a better life.

Then one day without warning, the firstborn son turned into an unmanageable boy, the "wild child." Unlike my younger sister, the "dream child," I frustrated every attempt my mother made to create the orderly, harmonious household she longed for.

I was never conscious of doing this deliberately, of course. In fact, what *I* longed for was to see a smile on my mother's face when she looked at me, instead of the stern gazes I remember – to feel her arms hugging me, instead of the stinging slap of her hand on my backside. But I had no clue how to gain her affection. Any attempt on my part seemed futile, like searching for a marble in a lake.

In a similar way, my mother didn't know how to reach me, to temper my "wildness" long enough to allow her to be the good mother she wanted to be. She was a young, inexperienced parent with two small children who were so completely different. Like me, she simply didn't know what to do.

Today, even though the causes and symptoms of ADHD are still being studied, many resources are emerging to help families cope with this condition: medical professionals and support groups; drug therapies and behavior management strategies; parenting workshops and individualized education plans; countless articles, books, and Web sites. None of these existed thirty years ago. Back then, ADHD kids and those with whom they struggled to have relationships were in the dark groping for answers.

My parents did the best they could with the knowledge and experience they had. I did the best I could, given the constraints of my condition. Thanks to the Lord, my parents and I now enjoy a great relationship, but the path leading to it was stony and uncertain. We stumbled a lot along the way, and at times still do. I don't think that's an unusual situation for most families, especially for families dealing with ADHD. We all struggle daily to find the hope in the hardship.

* * * * *

My mother was a stay-at-home mom. She provided for my sister's and my physical and spiritual needs, and even though she never showed a lot of affection, she told us she loved us, and we believed it.

But I always perceived that my mother *liked* my sister more than me. I'm sure part of it was sibling rivalry. Part of it may have been the way ADHD colored my point of view. But I think a larger part of it was that my sister was simply an easier child to deal with.

From my perspective – and keep in mind this is the perspective of an ADHD child who tends to feel things deeply without always sensing their causes and consequences – I was never good enough compared to my sister. When I did something wrong, I got punished. When my sister did something wrong, she was easily forgiven. My sister earned excellent grades at school; I didn't. My sister was socially popular; I wasn't. We were as opposite as opposites can get.

But mostly, I perceived that my mother treated us differently, and I didn't understand it. I resented it. I felt rejected by my peers at school and, even worse, by my own family. Like any big brother, I took out my anger and frustrations on my little sister. What feelings I couldn't resolve by harassing her, I internalized and used to fuel my downward spiraling self-esteem.

Several years ago while we were having a heart-to-heart talk, my mother revealed to me that she and my father didn't have a clue about to how to raise me. Like most parents, they were especially strict with their firstborn, and started to relax only when the next child came along.

On the other hand, I also presented special challenges that would have stumped most new parents of their generation. And because my father worked such long hours, the responsibility for doling out punishments went almost entirely to my mother.

From elementary school through high school, my mother dominated my life. While my sister seemed to enjoy many privileges, I was kept on a tight leash. The penalty for tugging on that leash was discipline. Admittedly, I was impulsive and didn't think things through before I did them. I was notorious for not looking both ways before crossing the street and for running in parking lots.

Looking back, I can see that *the leash* was more like a safety harness. My mother wanted to protect me, but at the time I only sensed the harshness of her discipline.

I actually feared my mother more than my father. In fact, my mother imposed such fear in my life that I truly believed she had the power to send me to hell. Ludicrous as that may seem, it was my reality as a young child.

As I grew older, our relationship grew more antagonistic. Once when I was being exceptionally defiant my mother slapped me. The sting of that slap stayed with me for many years. It reinforced my belief that my mother only desired to keep me in a cage and to never allow me to explore my independence.

In reality, she feared that giving me more freedom would lead to harm. My mother once witnessed several boys from my school pinning me to the ground and burning me with a cigarette lighter. The sting of that terrible sight stayed with her for many years.

So back and forth we went, a tug of war of wills. I tried hard to spread my wings. She tried just as hard to clip them. By the time I entered my early twenties and moved out of the house, I felt like a *neutral* person — a cardboard cutout of a grown man.

Today my mother regrets that she ever raised her hand to me; she wishes that she had handled many situations differently. She asked for my forgiveness, and I have forgiven her. I'm more understanding of why she parented me the way she did. And while my relationship with her was strained for many years, I can say without any hesitation that my mother also happens to be the greatest spiritual influence in my life. In spite of the mistakes she made as a parent, she turned to the Lord at a critical time in our lives and sought His wisdom. When she was saved, in a very real sense, our whole family was saved.

With the Lord's help, we have chosen not to dwell on the dark shadows of our past, but rather to focus on the positive aspects of our relationship today. There are many miles between us now, but my mom and I are very close. We call each other weekly and have deeply spiritual talks about the Lord. She has been patient with me, and has walked with me through the ups and downs of my life. I would never trade the relationship that I have with my mother today. I know that when the Lord calls my mother home, it will be great loss to me. My mom is tops in my book.

*****

My relationship with my father is also a bittersweet story. I didn't know my father growing up. We didn't really have a relationship. That feels odd to say because now our relationship is awesome. But when I was a child my father was a stranger to me.

He worked three jobs so that my mother could stay home. He wanted to make sure that my sister and I would never come home to an empty house; he and my mother both had experienced enough of that as children. So my father worked as a postman in the morning, a credit union representative in the afternoon, and a janitor in the evening.

He provided for us to the point that we could be considered a middle class family. We had clothes on our backs, three meals a day, a house, and two cars. For an Hispanic family, we were very well off compared to other families in the neighborhood.

My father was a good provider, but he was an absentee dad, emotionally and physically. When I did see him, he looked tired and upset. I don't recall him smiling, nor do I remember his eyes. He wore dark glasses a lot. My guess was he wore them to hide his anger, or maybe his sadness.

I have a few childhood memories of my dad that I will always treasure. I remember in elementary school where I got picked on frequently, my father occasionally came to school and stood at a distance in the play yard, keeping watch to make sure that I didn't get bullied.

One day he stayed with me for awhile in my kindergarten class. I don't recall how it happened, but somehow I cut my finger, and I remember my dad put a band-aid on it. *I cherished* that band-aid – that tiny, simple brown band-aid. Later in class, it came loose and fell off. I started sobbing and couldn't stop. In an attempt to fix the situation, my teacher threw out the old band-aid and put a new one on my finger. I cried even harder. She didn't understand why; nobody did.

At the time, I couldn't tell you why. But when my dad put on that band-aid, it was like a golden ring to me. I cherished that bandage as if my dad had given me the most precious treasure in the world. I felt completely devastated when it fell off, like someone had died. I was heartbroken, and I couldn't explain why.

I recall another time when my dad came home from work one night in an uncharacteristically happy mood. He walked through the door, and instead of going straight to the television, he surprised us all with a box of doughnuts. I don't remember the details of what we did; all I remember is that I liked being around him at that moment. He was approachable; he seemed happy, and he paid attention to me.

The next morning I happened to get up early while my father was getting ready for work. On my way to the bathroom, he met me in the hallway and, without a word, scooped me up and gave me a big bear hug. My dad rarely hugged me. To this day I can't describe fully how that embrace touched my heart. It was as if a spell had been cast. For one incredible moment, I was in heaven, nestled tightly in my father's arms.

Later that night when my father came home from work, I wondered if the spell would continue. As he entered the door, I looked up expectantly but quickly sensed a familiar tension. My father was in his usual cranky mood and immediately retreated to the television room. I kept my distance, as usual, and found something else to occupy my time with. The spell was broken.

Before my twelfth birthday, my dad did something I will never forget. There was a program in my church called the Royal Rangers, a Christian version of the boy scouts for fathers and sons. I wanted badly to join the Rangers with my father, and one evening at church while my father was in choir practice, I knelt down on the altar to pray and asked God to *please* let my dad agree to join the Royal Rangers with me.

I was praying hard and didn't hear my father come up behind me. He gently laid his hands on my shoulders and slowly, almost in a whisper, he asked the Lord to forgive him for not being a good father. I was stunned.

My father never verbalized his feelings. His spiritual life especially was a private matter; we never knew where he stood in his relationship with the Lord. At that moment, though, I detected a sense of utter defeat in my father's voice. I remained kneeling with my head down, unsure of what to do next. Then, just as he came, my father quietly walked away.

My father always seemed to be coming and going in our lives. When he came home from work, we had dinner together as a family, but my father ate quickly and bypassed all conversation so that he could retreat to the front room to watch his sports shows on television.

I began to resent sports because they stole my father's attention from me. I couldn't even watch television shows with a father-son theme without feeling a gnawing sense of disgust. Locked in the television set was everything I wished to be and to have and to share with my father, but never would.

Eventually, my resentment grew stronger. By the time I was 12, I hated my father. *Hate* is a strong word to use, I know, but at the time I detested him. I hated that I had his first name, Michael, as my middle name. I hated his last name. I hated that I resembled him. When I looked in the mirror I felt physically ill because I saw reflected in my own face the features of a man I didn't know.

My father remained a stranger to me until 1991. That year his mother, my grandmother, passed away. My father never knew his own father; he was killed in World War II, and his stepfather was an alcoholic who physically abused his wife and children. So my grandmother's death affected my father deeply.

By this time, I had already started my music ministry and was traveling quite a bit. My father called me to tell me about my grandmother's death, and then he asked me a question that shocked me: "David Michael, would you sing at your grandmother's funeral?"

My father knew I was in the ministry, but he had never shared with me how he felt about it. I didn't know if he approved or disapproved. But here, suddenly, my dad was asking me to sing – to provide the only music – at my grandmother's funeral. If the president of the United States had asked me to sing at that moment, it couldn't have been a higher honor.

The funeral was packed. I was surprised by how many people knew my father and grandmother. My father's co-workers from the post office were there, dressed in uniform and occupying six entire rows of pews. It moved me to see so many people come to show their support. Throughout the service, one after another of my father's co-workers came up to me to tell me how impressed they were by my singing and how my father always bragged about me - *bragged about me*. My father bragged about me? I couldn't believe it.

All of my father's siblings and step-siblings were there, too. I listened intently as they recounted many stories of how my father had taken care of the family. Their stepfather was a terrible man. He had deceived my grandmother and married her while he was still married to another woman in Mexico. When his first wife died, he brought all of his children to live with my grandmother and father.

It was my father who had protected the entire family from the alcoholic rages of their stepfather. Whenever their stepfather went on a drunken rampage, my father was the one who would keep the younger children calm and out of harm's way, quietly slipping them out of the house if necessary.

The conversation continued to twist and turn. I learned my father was a devoutly religious man. He was raised Catholic, and every Sunday, bible in hand, he took the entire family to church. He went to parochial schools and at one time wanted to become a priest. He wanted to go into the ministry!

I couldn't believe what I was hearing. I sat perfectly still not wanting to disrupt the flow of conversation around me. There was so much I never knew about my father. And now, after twenty years, I was finally starting to understand. I was becoming acquainted with *the man* who was my father.

At the cemetery I stood proudly beside my father like a soldier. Silently and resolutely, my father had faced so many battles in his life, and now, as we laid my grandmother to rest, I knew he was bravely enduring another.

I laid my head on his shoulder. To my surprise, he laid his head on mine. We held each other, and without exchanging a word, the years of bitterness and resentment gently slipped away. From that moment on, my father was a hero to me.

Several years later, on the heels of another ministry tour, I flew home to California to be with my family for Christmas. My father met me at the airport and on an impulse I offered to treat him to dinner. He accepted, and we had a nice, long drive to the restaurant, where we talked easily for the first time without any lapse in conversation.

As I had dinner with my father, I suddenly felt like that little boy in the hallway, surprised by a big, strong bear hug from his daddy. It was a moment that will always stay with me — a "band-aid moment," if you will.

When the world has come against me
And it seems like I cannot make it at all
Help me Lord to take my eyes off the Jericho walls
And help me Lord to keep my eyes on you

From the song *Trust In You*
(David Michael Carrillo © 1989 The Songs of GentleWind)

David Michael Carrillo

CHAPTER 4
The Caged Bird Sings

*...Show me the way I should go,
for to you I lift up my soul.*
Psalm 143:8

In my parents' backyard in Whittier, CA, a heap of rusty metal lays where my swing set used to be. A beautiful garden surrounds it now, some thirty years later. Very little is left of the yard I knew as a boy. I remember swinging for hours on that swing set, back and forth, like a caged bird, trying to forget the past or look toward some kind of future.

I knew at the age of eight years, the night I saw Jeff Steinberg and his Masterpiece in Progress revival, that my future would be the music ministry. So, strangely enough, figuring out what God wanted me to do with my life was easy. The hard part was figuring out how to trust God enough to lead me to that ministry in His own time, in His own way.

My song *He Flew Away* describes the exhilarating freedom of taking a step of faith and then seeing God take you places you never imagined. For me, finding my way off the swing and beyond the challenges of ADHD has been difficult. Throughout most of my childhood, I swung back and forth in my so-called cage uncertain of which way to go, sometimes leaping toward, and, to be honest, sometimes steering clear of the open door.

* * * * *

When I was 10 years old, I took a leap of faith that nearly crushed my spirit. After spending five long years doing literally nothing in the educably handicapped (EH) class, I decided I'd had enough. Every day I watched my peers in that class go nowhere. They kept getting in trouble at school and ultimately with the law. I was convinced I wasn't learning anything, and that if I didn't do something soon, I would end up like them. So I fought with my teachers and with the school district to get me into a "regular" classroom.

In the fall of 1976 my work paid off, and I was placed in a standard fifth-grade classroom with nearly 30 students – 30, not 12! My first day of class was like a dream come true. I remember walking into the classroom as the bell rang, taking my seat, and soaking up everything and everyone around me. I couldn't stop grinning. With great relief I thought, "Hey, I'm normal now. I'm normal!"

The rude awakening came when my teacher asked us to open our books. I looked down and couldn't make sense of any of the words on the page. *I didn't know how to read.* I was panic stricken! As I heard the class read aloud, I pretended to follow along, determined not to let anyone see my fear. The only thing I could comprehend at that moment was the sick feeling in the pit of my stomach as I realized how far behind I was academically from my peers.

The first time a kid ever called me stupid was in the EH class, but the first time I ever *felt* stupid was in that "regular" fifth-grade classroom. I truly struggled in that class. I didn't even know how to spell Michael, my middle name, yet every night I was assigned homework. I was expected to read and to write and to produce. Only by the grace of God, I kept moving forward. My work wasn't great, but I managed to do well enough to stay in regular classes. Going back to the EH class was not an option for me.

Fearfully and Wonderfully Made

* * * * *

In 1978 I entered the sixth grade, and the struggles continued. That year my teachers, once again, were concerned about my hyperactivity and my inability to interact with my peers. After several consultations with my teachers and parents, my psychiatrist decided I should be hospitalized for a month so that the doctors could determine the best combination of drugs to help "calm" me.

As I checked into the hospital, I felt the cage crash down around me. The doctors tried all kinds of medications, but again, nothing worked. The drugs made me groggy instead of more focused. After thirty days, I remained a mystery to my frustrated doctors.

Upon my return to school, my classmates bombarded me with questions about where I had been. I kept my story a mystery to them as well. It was far better than bearing the humiliation of telling the truth.

One bright spot emerged during those grim days. My sixth-grade teacher who played guitar organized a spring concert that included my class and two others. Auditions were announced for a solo, which, strange as it may seem, I didn't hesitate to try out for. To my amazement, I got the lead part. I was picked to sing the song *Lean on Me*, accompanied by my teacher on guitar.

At my very first concert performance, I stood on stage in front of a microphone and sang my heart out to an audience. (Those "silly" first-grade sketches had come to life!) That concert was another moment of truth for me. I realized singing was my destiny. The concert was also my first introduction to guitar music, which I discovered I loved as much as singing.

By the seventh grade, I was in the chorus and music was taking shape in my life. It didn't matter that I was a geeky kid with bony fingers and a high-pitched voice. I had found my niche and started to pursue it with a passion.

But there was also school, which I hated with a passion. My freshman year in high school turned out to be a terrible, terrible year. I struggled academically, no surprise. I was also picked on and beat up. The greatest blow, however, came when I tried out for a small ensemble group and didn't make it. Just as quickly as the dream came, it departed from my life. From that point on, the year grew progressively worse. My parents decided the best solution was to put me in a different school.

* * * * *

In the fall of 1981 I started my sophomore year at California High, where I stayed until graduation. Being able to start over was refreshing. I had a clean slate, an open door. My sophomore year was the only school year I would ever recall fondly, thanks to my drama teacher and choir teacher, who led the school's ensemble group.

While I didn't make the ensemble group my freshman year, I made it at my new school, surprisingly as a bass singer (I'm a first tenor). The group was a show choir, which meant that I gained the opportunity to learn about the drama of musical performances as well as timing in acting. This helped me tremendously later in my career when I would do television shows and radio spots.

I also started to observe more closely the work of Richard Crain, who was the music director at the First Family Assembly of God, the church where I was raised. He directed the church choir and orchestra as well as a praise band. Back in the 70s and early 80s, praise and worship bands like Seek Ye First and I Love You, Lord, were just breaking ground.

Richard was classically trained and introduced our church to the beauty of traditional hymns as well as to praise and worship music. I would ultimately do several tours with Richard, including a Pacific Northwest tour in the summer of 1982. I remember that tour vividly because it was one of the best choirs our church had at the time – it was also the first time I experienced real *friendship*.

On the ferry boat ride from Prince Rupert, Canada, to Juneau, Alaska, I met a new group of kids outside of the usual circle I knew from school and church. We talked, laughed, sang, and just hung out together. We all clicked, which baffled me. Until then, I had only experienced people from a distance.

But on that tour, which was also my first exposure to the music ministry, I felt accepted as part of a community of friends. I'll never forget that feeling. Coincidentally, on the heels of that tour, I bought a record album to check out a new song that I liked, and came to experience the remarkable music of another Christian artist, Nancy Honeytree, who to this day remains one of my dearest friends.

* * * * *

Nancy's music touched my heart at that time in a way no other music did. She wrote about her personal fears and doubts, feelings I could relate to, yet her profound love for the Lord, then and now, has always been revealed clearly in her music.

Two songs affected me deeply. The opening lines from her song "Honeytree" spoke to the doubts I was experiencing then about my own self worth:

> *Somehow, let me see who I am.*
> *I see who I am not,*
> *See what I haven't got.*
> *So who am I?*

Who was I? I had been told I was a mistake, worthless, unwanted. Was that the truth? Or was there a reason for my life that held value? Another of Nancy's songs, "Diamond in the Rough," gave me hope that the latter might be true:

> *Someday you will be*
> *A polished living stone,*
> *Though now you are*
> *A diamond in the rough.*

My mother often referred to me as a diamond in the rough. The notion that the Lord was still working in my life, and that maybe He was molding something meaningful out of my ADHD – well, to me, that was a fantastic discovery. I branded my soul with that idea and used it to carry me through the later part of high school. Nancy's music was a lifesaver to me during those difficult years.

I currently serve on Nancy's ministry board in Indiana and visit with her family often. In January 2004, a life-long dream came to pass when we collaborated on a two-day concert together in Sheboygan, Wisconsin. (As a matter of fact, we sang a duet of both "Honeytree" and "Diamond in the Rough!") Nancy has been a true friend through the years, and much like my mother, she is a great spiritual mentor.

It is a joyful feeling for someone with ADHD to be able to call another person *friend*. Building relationships is incredibly hard when you have trouble recognizing or responding to normal social cues, or when you're emotionally five to ten years behind other kids your age. Looking back on my childhood, I can't recall having a single close friend.

Sadly, for some children with ADHD, the inability to cultivate friendships leads to lifelong hardship – and sometimes to tragic consequences. I remain grateful to that Pacific Northwest tour for many things, but mostly for introducing me to the joy of friendship. Today I count my friends among the greatest of God's blessings in my life.

*****

My junior and senior years in high school were regrettably the most awful, hellish years of my childhood. I suffered terribly academically, but I struggled more in my relationship with my mother.

In my junior year I was just beginning to wrestle with the normal physical and emotional changes that most kids experience at the age of 11 or 12. I was trying to develop personal relationships outside the home. I even fell in love with a beautiful girl.

My mother, as I shared earlier, kept a tight leash on me. The more independent I tried to become, the more discipline she imposed upon me. From her perspective, giving me more freedom was akin to feeding me to the wolves. Too many times she had witnessed me getting beaten and harassed by other kids at school, and even at church.

Of course, I wasn't aware of my mother's concerns regarding my safety. I was only tuned in to my own point of view, which was simply this: my mother had become a prison warden who took great delight in smothering the slightest sparks of freedom in my life. I rebelled. We fought constantly. Our conflicts affected the whole family.

To further complicate matters, some of my mom's Christian friends who had witnessed our struggles came up to me privately and said, "David Michael, you need to stand up to your mother." This shocked me. I was always taught that you should honor your father and mother. Yet here were grown adults in our church, whom I had respected, telling me to challenge my own mother! I became confused. I didn't know what was right or wrong. I didn't know who I was or what to believe.

In my senior year, I broke up with my high school sweetheart. During the course of an argument, she slapped me. I was devastated; I couldn't believe that she hit me. The only person who had ever slapped me was my mother. I automatically reached the conclusion that by slapping me my girlfriend was trying to assume a position of authority over me equal to my mother.

The relationship quickly fell apart after that. It was such a mess that our parents had to get involved. In so many ways, I wish I had handled that situation differently. But I had no sense of how to navigate the maze of emotional conflicts that for most kids is just normal teen angst.

*****

As I mentioned earlier, Nancy Honeytree's music pulled me through many difficult times in my high school years. In the summer of 1983, feeling that I had someone I could look up to, I started to teach myself how to play the guitar. I had found my role model in the music ministry and wanted to follow in her steps.

My junior and senior English literature teacher also played an important role in getting me started in the ministry. A devoutly Christian woman working in the public school system, she quickly sensed my low self-esteem when I entered her class. She was one of the first teachers who desired to help me cultivate my musical gifts.

She taught me to write poetry, and through her encouragement, during my junior year I wrote my very first song, "*TV.*" It was a simple ballad about the sorrows of a lost childhood.

> *A long time ago, there's this boy that I know,*
> *who sat quietly watching the TV.*
>
> *I know him very well, because I am he,*
> *I am that boy who watched too much TV.*
> *TV, you stole my life away,*
> *you told me lies, and then*
> *you robbed me of my childhood days.*

It got an A+ - the first I ever received!

In my senior year, I wrote "We Are One in the Son," which is now on one of my CDs. It was during my senior year when things began to change for me. I dragged my guitar everywhere, playing between class breaks and free periods. One day in English class, my teacher without warning asked me to share a song with my classmates. I was startled. The kids, of course, immediately mocked me and said, "Yeah, yeah, play us a song."

My teacher looked at me expectantly. Mustering every bit of courage I had, I walked to the front of the room, picked up my guitar, and began to sing. I don't remember the song; I only remember the looks on the kids' faces, including the big, tough football players. Some of them were actually in tears. When I finished the song there was silence. At that moment, I realized my music affected people.

After that day many of the kids started to treat me a little differently. I can't say I was ever fully accepted. Nobody was patting me on the back or inviting me to be best friends. But I noticed a subtle change, as if some of the kids were thinking, "Hey, you're okay" or "That's kind of neat." My music was beginning to open doors for me. In turn, I began to take bigger leaps of faith.

> *Then one day the cage was left open*
> *The songbird saw that this was his chance to escape*
> *On the window ledge*
> *The sun seemed to welcome him*
> *Wings stretched out to catch the morning rays*
> *And he hears the wind call his name*
> *Come and fly away*
>
> From the song *He Flew Away*
> (David Michael Carrillo © 2005 The Songs of GentleWind)

CHAPTER 5
Betrayal

Save me, O God, for the waters have come up to my neck....
I have come into the deep waters; the floods engulf me.
Psalm 69:1-2

People with ADHD, especially children, feel certain things deeply. You may not see it in them; they may not be able to show it, but it's true.

The web of human emotions is wide and intricate. When a stressful life event collides with that web or tugs on a strand of it, the vibrations are clearly felt yet fairly well contained by most people. For persons with ADHD, however, the vibrations, no matter how slight, can agitate our psyches like the aftershocks of an earthquake. Whether events or people's intentions merit it, we can attach great emotional highs or lows to a random act, a silent pause, or a brief glance.

An important life skill for persons with ADHD is learning how to manage their emotional responses to situations. This involves being able to perceive the real intentions of people's words and actions, as well as being able to moderate one's reactions to them. It's like learning how to tune the strings of a guitar to produce the truest sound. It's not an impossible task for someone with ADHD, but it does require patience and concentration, and lots of practice.

* * * * *

Although music prompted me to take bigger steps of faith in my young life, patience and concentration were not my greatest strengths. They weren't even on the radar screen. A consuming passion for my music ministry was the focal point of my life.

My first ministry experience was singing once a month in a convalescent home. It was the highlight of my life in 1983, and through it I learned to play traditional hymns. In 1984 my ministry experience escalated suddenly and dramatically. In February I went to an all-district church youth camp in Big Bear, California, and was asked to play my song *We Are One in the Son* in front of 500 attendees.

The song was a hit! I still have a recording of that day that includes both my performance and my efforts to teach the song to all the campers. The singing combined with the interaction with the kids was so gratifying. I discovered that in addition to performing, I enjoyed reaching out and connecting with an audience. Soon after that event I was flooded with offers to lead worship for my youth group and other church camps. All the new attention was exciting.

That summer after graduation, I went on my last youth choir tour. We traveled the East Coast from New York City to Orlando, Florida. I thrived on the busy travel schedules and the encounters with so many different people. But, to be completely honest, I found the tour especially appealing for one other reason: I had a solo performance. I loved being in the spotlight – it energized me! Each morning I jumped out of bed wide awake, ready for the next city, the next show.

One early morning in North Carolina as I watched the sunrise, I whispered a quiet prayer to the Lord. "This is what I want to do, Lord. I want to travel and sing for you."

Only 24 hours before when I shared this dream with two of my peers from the youth choir, I was told, "David, give it up; your music is outdated. I can do circles around you easily."

Another voice piped in, "Yeah, David, who wants to listen to your 'hippy' music." Their words pierced me like arrows. I couldn't believe that I was being verbally attacked by people close to me, people who, like me, were supposed to be serving the Lord through their gifts of music. But their opinions, however painful to hear, didn't dissuade me. I was on a spiritual high and ready to discover the next adventure that God had in store for me.

1985 brought another exciting turning point in my life. In January I auditioned for and was accepted to be part of a new recording called *Hi-Tops* with Maranatha! Music. The creative energy of working in a recording studio fueled my songwriting aspirations, and I got down to business. Under Nancy Honeytree's influence I also learned to write folk music, which I consider to be my musical roots and the basis for many of my personal experience songs.

I began to do more local ministry, but I was eager to find a way to get back on the road. In June of 1985 my prayers were answered. An up-and-coming evangelist asked me if I would lead the worship and share in the special music at a revival service he was conducting. It was to be held in Derby Acres, California, three hours away from my home town of Whittier. I was excited – my first "long-distance" trip as a solo singer!

The evangelist and I arrived Friday night and held our first service on Saturday. It was well received. On Sunday morning, I went for a prayer walk to prepare for the morning service. It was during that walk that the Lord spoke to my heart. "David Michael, would you be willing to leave the comfort of home and serve me here?"

I stopped, looked around, and saw nothing but dirt. Derby Acres is in the high California desert and land locked. No trees, no beach, no Disneyland – just dirt. Yet my reply to the Lord's words were: "I guess so Lord, if that's what you want." Now, why did I say that out loud, I thought, as I walked along? How strange for me to have these thoughts. Why would I move to a place like this anyway?

Later that night after evening service, the pastor asked me if I would consider staying in Derby Acres for awhile and helping with the ministry there. I guess the Lord was preparing me to respond confidently to that request. And so, I stayed five months as a youth leader and music minister. The pastor was 20 years old, the associate pastor was 19, and I was 19. There we were, three young boys leading a church where the people in the congregation were on average 40 years of age! Fortunately, the three of us worked very well as a team, and the congregation seemed to accept us.

You learn a lot from sheer life experience, and through my experience at that small little white church in Derby Acres, I learned much of my ministry practicum – by simply doing it. But that environment was a real test of my spiritual and emotional maturity, which I quickly discovered was in its infancy. We witnessed heart-wrenching cases of child abuse. I personally had to turn in a father for beating his child. We conducted a funeral for an infant who drowned in a swimming pool. I wrote a song for that service and interacted closely with the grief-stricken family. We dealt with fornication, pregnancies out of wedlock, drug addictions. Our responses to these situations were learned on the spot. It was "on the job training" like I had never experienced. Many of the hard lessons learned I still keep with me today.

One of those lessons came from the pastor. My enthusiasm for *my music* sometimes got the better of me, and I remember one day the pastor approached me and said very directly: "David Michael, I don't need a ham-up singer, I need a humble servant. You're here to minister to the people, not to do a show. You're here to bless their hearts, not yours. You're here for them; they're not here for you. Once you learn that, you'll be a powerful minister." It was not the easiest thing to hear at the time, but those words have guided my ministry for many years.

*****

That summer I wrote many of the songs that appeared on my first album: *Trust In You, I Surrender, I Rejoice*. That was the same summer I was introduced to the music of John Michael Talbot, a popular Christian musician and author. John Michael's music is considered sacred and meditative in style, and this was also a great influence to me at the time.

After my service at Derby Acres, I embarked on my first overseas ministry in England. For two weeks in April 1987 as part of a ministry team I performed at schools, rest homes, and church revivals. It was exhilarating, and I knew I wanted to keep pursuing that kind of traveling music ministry. As a result, I moved away from Whittier, California, and became involved with Calvary Chapel in Costa Mesa, California. Working with Calvary, the third largest church in America, gave me great exposure, and I soon felt like everything was finally coming together for me.

Over the next few years I grew spiritually and musically in my ministry. I led praise and worship services at Calvary Chapel and worked alongside pastors at weddings and funerals. I became actively involved in a home study group, which was an important source of fellowship and support for me during my early ministry. I conducted my first solo tour and was privileged to work with two more musical mentors, Christian music artists Terry Talbot and Wendy Francisco. I landed a contract with a record company and recorded my first solo album, *In The Quiet Moments*, which was later released by ASAPH Records. To my own surprise, I even found time to meet a wonderful girl, and we became engaged to be married.

God was good! I had responded totally and joyfully to His call to the music ministry. In return, He blessed my life abundantly. I was on my way, personally and professionally. I was living on my own, young and in love, happily immersed in God's work. When it all came crashing down around me I was completely unprepared.

*****

In 1991 the record company that signed me for my first album went bankrupt and dropped me. I started my own label, GentleWind Music, but business was painfully slow to develop. In another stinging blow, my relationship with my fiancée crumbled, and we called off the engagement. The feelings of rejection that held me hostage throughout my childhood started to entrap me again.

The greatest shock of all came from the most unexpected source. Several senior members of my church, with whom I had shared my deepest feelings about recent events, broadcast and twisted those confidences in a chain of gossip that reverberated throughout the congregation. Their betrayal – which I perceived to be an outright rejection of my trust – shattered my faith. A tidal wave of rejection and betrayal hit me without warning. What on earth did I do to deserve this?

With no one else to turn to, I turned to God, although in utter defeat. I wasn't looking for strength or reasons why. My words amounted to this: "Lord, I'm sick of the church, I'm sick of being backstabbed, I'm sick of being rejected. Therefore, I'm going to do my own thing now. I don't live with my parents anymore, and there's a whole world I've never experienced. I'm going to do what *I want* now. So, Lord, here's how it is. I'm going to ask you to be merciful to me, gracious to me, and watch out for me because I know I'm going to be bad and go the other way. So all I can ask is that you be kind to me and bring me back to you when it's time."

That was my prayer. It was all I could manage. I packed my bags and moved to Portland, Oregon.

In my afflictions
And in my distress
I'll stand still
And I will see
Your faithfulness

From the song *Wounds and Pain*
(David Michael Carrillo © 2002 The Songs of GentleWind)

David Michael Carrillo

CHAPTER 6
The Prodigal Son

I have strayed like a lost sheep.
Psalm 119:176

When I moved to Portland in the later part of 1991, I discovered that the physical distance created a bigger gap between my mother and me. I knew that my living so far away was breaking her heart. At the same time, I didn't let myself care about how she felt, as harsh as that sounds. The realization that nearly 1,000 miles meant she was no longer able to control my life was liberating.

I still called her and told her about the new things I was doing. She listened and told me she loved me, but I could tell our relationship was changing. I was becoming more independent. She was starting to let go.

Like the phone calls to my mother, I made token gestures to stay involved with church. I visited many churches but noticed quickly that much of Portland and its Christian communities were very liberal in their beliefs. I had always been raised to think one way about Christianity. All of a sudden I was hearing other perspectives.

There were doctrines on pre-Rapture, post-Rapture, no-Rapture, pre-millenialism, post-millenialism, once saved-always saved, abuse it-lose it. Some churches believed in the authority of scripture; others presented the Bible as nothing more than a good moral book; still others emphasized its historical flaws and literary devices, and so it went.

So many points of view, and all claimed they were right! I was confused and began to question everything. I didn't even know if I believed in the Bible anymore. Then one day in March of 1992, I just stopped questioning. I finally told the Lord, "Look, you can have it all. I'm done."

I stopped going to church. However, I didn't stop believing in God, or in His love for me. In fact, God's love for me was the only thing I didn't question. People are surprised to learn that I wrote the song *Jesus Loves Me* during this period of my life. For me it was simply a testament to the one tiny seed of faith I still clung to – although, it still wasn't enough to make this prodigal son return home.

* * * * *

Without the shadow of parental or church authorities hovering over me, I tried it all. I didn't do drugs, but I did the club and bar scenes. I hung out with the "wrong crowds" and experimented with all the social taboos – alcohol, body piercing, hair dyeing, you name it. I was on a mission to find my wild oats and sow them all.

The irony was startling. While doing everything that church and family preached against, I suddenly became popular. I had a phone list of friends I could call and socialize with at a moment's notice. I learned how to stand up for myself and to push back when confronted.

This was incredible! My church rejected me, but my "hoodlum" friends welcomed me, accepted me, without any conditions. They showed more Christian concern for my well being than the supposed *true* Christians who betrayed me.

So here I was in this strange situation – feeling pretty good about myself and my new life, yet also feeling agitated because in the deep recesses of my mind I could still sense the presence of the Holy Spirit. I knew this wasn't the life God had in store for me, but I didn't want to go back.

Going back meant allowing myself to be ridiculed, rejected, stepped on. I learned that when you're in the ministry you're always a target for some back pew archer who's ready to shoot you down for whatever reason. You're loved by some and hated by others. I didn't want to be someone's punching bag, so I fought back.

I put away my guitar, but that didn't stop *the call*, which by then had been orbiting around me like a humming mosquito. After I had stashed away my guitar, I received a phone call from a Christian radio station that knew of my music (it was still being played on the air even though I was no longer playing it).

The station learned I was living in Portland and wanted to do an interview. I somewhat reluctantly agreed. The station was excited to have me on the show and asked me about all the events that inspired the songs I had written. It was one of the strangest moments I have ever experienced. I felt like a huge hypocrite. There I was talking like a Christian and living like the devil!

That night in bed I lay awake pondering the contrary life I was living. I didn't see it then, but I know now that when you belong to the Lord, you can run away as far as you want, as fast as you want, in any direction, but you always end up running right back to Him because He's with you all the time. You can turn your back, you can harden your heart, yet still He waits.

* * * * *

Early one Saturday morning I stumbled into my apartment still tipsy from a party the night before and thought I'd take a break before heading out again later that night. I turned on the television. A children's show was on the Trinity Broadcasting Network (TBN), a popular 24-hour faith channel. The show looked kind of cute, so I sat back and kicked up my feet. The show was the *Bible Club*, or something like that, and it featured the story of "Jonah and the Whale."

A woman was narrating the story of the prophet Jonah to a group of children gathered around her. The camera closed in on her as she talked about how God had called Jonah, but Jonah decided instead to go his own way. God allowed Jonah to go only so far before He imposed His will upon him. Jonah was tossed out of the boat in which he had tried to escape, swallowed by the whale, and ultimately taken back in the direction God wanted him to go. Jonah washed ashore unharmed and obediently set off to do God's will.

I sat motionless, my eyes glued to the television screen. The camera slowly pulled back, and the woman narrating the story paused for a moment. She looked straight into the camera, pointed her finger, and said, "Don't be a Jonah. Do God's will."

The awesome childlike faith I had experienced in my first-grade Sunday school class suddenly washed over me. My heart felt full, and tears welled in my eyes. When the woman on television pointed her finger at the screen, I felt like she was pointing directly at me. I fell to the floor sobbing.

"What am I doing with my life?" I cried. "Lord, I'm Jonah. I'm going in the wrong direction and sinking fast. You gotta help me, Lord."

I cried a long time. Then, I knew what I had to do. I picked up the phone and called my mom. It was the call she had been praying for. I told her I was done with the world and wanted to go back to the Lord.

"I don't know what to expect, Mom," I said, "but I want to be with God's people again. Even though I don't trust them yet, I know I'd rather be with the Lord than to have fame, friends, and acceptance. If I don't have the Lord, then all of that is in vain."

After I hung up with my mom, I called my friend, Pastor Doug Snow of Calvary Chapel South Portland and told him where I had been and what was going on with my life. "Look, Doug," I said, "I don't want to be in the ministry or to forge any church relationship. All I want is just to sit and hear God's word again. That's all."

Without any hesitation, he invited me to visit his church. From that point forward, I immersed myself in God's word and God's people. Hearing God's word again was like basking in warm sunshine. And to my surprise, the church community welcomed me with open arms. I was lovingly accepted by the people, but I was still apprehensive.

* * * * *

In September 1993, Trinity Broadcasting Network called me and asked me to share my music on the program *Joy in the Morning*. ("How ironic," I thought, yet again.) I was surprised that TBN was even familiar with my music.

Apparently, some of my recordings had gained the attention of one of the producers, who invited me to do the show. But it had been only one month since I had returned to the Lord, so I was a bit hesitant about doing the program. I recalled how hypocritical I felt during the last radio interview I had given.

David Michael Carrillo

I shared my concerns with my friend, Doug. He was entirely supportive and encouraged me to do the show. I could never have known then that my guest appearance on TBN would be the beginning of a completely new direction in my life and ministry. Slowly, I took another step of faith.

Lord, my life to you I bring
I lay it down at your feet
Help me be faithful to you
Like a bride who weds her groom
Lord, I pledge my love to you
Help me be faithful to you

From the song *Faithful*
(David Michael Carrillo © 1990/2005 The Songs of GentleWind)

CHAPTER 7
Searching For Home

The Lord is with me; I will not be afraid.
What can man do to me?
Psalm 118:6

My walk back to the Lord was a slow one. My friend, Doug Snow, took me under his wing and nursed my spiritual health. He knew I was called to the ministry, but he also understood I was a bit shell-shocked, so he started slow, gradually giving me small tasks within his congregation.

By December 1993, I was singing fairly regularly and leading worship activities. Still, I wasn't motivated to look for new challenges. I was content to nibble on the small ministerial duties Doug tossed my way.

During this time I suffered another failed relationship – another rejection. Why did I seem destined to face one rejection after another? I understood that God gives everyone the free will to make their own choices, but, why, I wondered, why does He allow me to make choices that He knows will hurt me? I was making an effort to come back to Him, but instead of getting stronger, I felt hopelessly weak.

I remember saying out loud, "I love you, Lord, but I do not trust you. If you want me in your ministry and you need me to be vulnerable, then you're asking the wrong person because I don't like being vulnerable."

I was hurting, but I was also unwilling to walk away from the Lord a second time. That would be admitting total defeat. I remained at Calvary Chapel South Portland, although I led a sort of solitary co-existence with the congregation, using the church like a cocoon to shelter me from the harsh elements of life.

* * * * *

The fine, silken strands that encased my cocoon was my music. Although my personal finances were a wreck, my record label, GentleWind Music, was still solvent, and I met two people who encouraged me to write and record music again.

John Conrad, an assistant pastor at a Lutheran church in South Portland, financed the recording of my second and third albums, *The Carols of Christmas* (1995) and *Journey with the Wind* (1996). He was so convinced of my musical ability that even I had to wonder what I might be missing if I didn't pursue it more aggressively. It also felt great to be in the recording studio again.

In the summer of 1995, just a few months before my Christmas album was to be released, John told me that he had been asked to establish a new church in central Indiana. He had decided to leave Portland. I understood this was a task he felt called to do, but it was difficult to see him go; he was a good friend.

Soon after John left, I made a television appearance on a local TBN station in Portland. One of the station engineers who knew John well joined me for a cup of coffee during a program break.

"So what happens if God asks you to move to Indiana, too?" he asked.

"Absolutely, not," I shot back. "I will not go. Portland is my home now."

"But what if it's God's perfect will?" he asked.

"No. I believe in free will, and I believe that God wants me in Portland. I'm going to stay right here!" I spoke these words firmly and deliberately, winding myself ever more securely within the soft casing of my cocoon.

When my Christmas album was released, I sent a few copies to John who told me that he was eager to give them away as Christmas presents to some of the Lutheran pastors he was working with in the Indianapolis area. Consequently, those pastors expressed great interest in my music, and in February 1996 John invited me to Indianapolis to help him celebrate the first service he officiated in his new church. While I was there he also arranged for me to do a concert tour of several of the Lutheran churches in the area.

The community of Lutheran churches welcomed me warmly, and later that summer, I was invited to Indianapolis again for another concert tour and to serve as a guest musician for several vacation bible study programs. The next couple of years became a very busy time, and I was amazed by the doors that were opening for me.

During 1996-97, I relocated for a short time to Vancouver, Washington, just 10 miles north of Portland, thanks to the support of another great friend, Jason Ritchie, who serves as assistant pastor and music director for Crossroads Community Church. Crossroads has an exceptional music program and over the years has helped to produce praise-and-worship tracks for churches in the Portland, Oregon, area and throughout the country. Back in 1996 Jason invited me to help him with the music program while I was recording my third album, *Journey with the Wind*. As the saying goes, it was an offer I couldn't refuse.

As I crossed the Columbia River, driving the short distance from Portland to Vancouver, I noticed instantly how different the two cities seemed. Vancouver *felt* like Indianapolis. Unlike Portland, which to me had always seemed like a playground for freethinking spirits, Vancouver and Indiana seemed more reminiscent of the traditional Christian communities I grew up with in Whittier, California. Although I wasn't consciously aware of it then, I think that Vancouver served as a staging ground for my eventual move to Indianapolis, which remains my home today.

At that time, of course, I still had no intention of moving to Indiana. I spent 1996 through 1997 dashing merrily from Portland, to Vancouver, to Indianapolis, on concert tours and summer vacation bible study programs. My ministry spread like wildfire. The CD versions of my *Carols of Christmas* and *Journey with the Wind* albums came out, and I was getting national air play again.

I had taken off on another fun roller coaster ride, cruising comfortably on the rails, and as usual, totally blind to the hairpin curve that lay ahead. Once I spied it, however, there was no turning back. I was soon to be derailed by a sweet family named the Strohm's: Carl and Jeanette, and their three sons, Jason, Justin, and Josh.

* * * * *

In 1997 I returned to Indiana for a six-week summer tour. The Strohm family welcomed me into their home for this particular tour. And I was excited to discover that they were (and still are today) a musical family, which was a special treat.

Their son Jason is an excellent guitar player, and, like me, had a lot of creative energy. Together we worked in the recording studio all summer on a song called "Lamb of God" (which was later released on my *A Pilgrim's Progress* CD).

Every other Saturday, Grandma and Grandpa Strohm, and Uncle David and Uncle Paul, came over, and brought their instruments: fiddles, banjos, and mandolins. They loved to play Appalachian and Bluegrass music, and I played along on my guitar, trying my best to keep up with them. We jammed together for several hours at a time and then capped off the evening with a big meal. All of the Strohm's made me feel like part of the family. It had been a long time since I had felt that close to a family.

Toward the end of my summer tour in Indianapolis, I traveled with the Strohm's to a Christian concert, an Upmost For His Highest concert. It was an awesome event, and when it was all over we headed home, tired but content, down a long stretch of highway back to the south side of Indianapolis.

The sun was setting, and I watched it cast a beautiful golden hue upon the passing corn fields that decorated mile after mile of roadside on I-69. As I looked out the window I thought to myself, "Gosh, this place is so different." And the Lord at that moment spoke to my heart and said, "You know where I want you now, don't you?"

I sat quietly in the back seat, and continued to stare out the window. The golden stalks became blurry as my eyes welled with tears. He went on, "I need you to be here in Indiana. You're going to be based in Indianapolis. And not only will you do your ministry here, but it's from here that I'm going to send you all over the world. From here your ministry will grow and multiply."

I wasn't surprised by these words. In my heart I knew the Lord had been preparing me to hear them since my move to

Vancouver, but I still hesitated. I wondered if the words might be an illusion. How could I trust that they were true?

I told the Lord, "That's great, *but*....there are some big obstacles to this plan, and if this is really you, Lord, then I'll give you three days to help me with those obstacles."

As I saw it, three obstacles stood between me and God's plan. First, where would I live? Except for the Strohm's, I didn't know anyone in the area, and I'd definitely need a roommate to make ends meet. Second, I would need a phone number and a post office box, which requires a legal residence. And finally, I would need to open a bank account – which was perhaps the biggest obstacle of all.

Back in my rebellious Portland days, I mismanaged my finances to the point that I had to file for bankruptcy, so my bank records and credit were a mess. In fact, I still owed the bank money for my personal checking account, and because of that I could not open a personal account anywhere in the country. Only my business account was still active.

I thought, surely that's going to be a huge problem, Lord. The next morning I called my bank in Portland to find out if there was anything I could do to resolve the situation.

The bank clerk was very pleasant. "Well, Mr. Carrillo, at one time our ledger showed that you owed $300, but according to our current records, the deficit has been taken care of. You don't owe us any money. You're clean and clear, so we'll take this off your record, and you can open a new account immediately with any bank."

I was dumbfounded. I knew for a fact that I didn't pay the money back, but somehow someone somewhere took care of it. Already – there was one obstacle solved.

A day later, I went downstairs to the family room in the Strohm house, and found Jeanette moving furniture around. "What are you doing?" I asked.

"We're just getting things ready," she said.

"Ready for what?" I asked.

"For when you move here," she said.

Now, I hadn't told anyone what was going on in my heart. I wondered, "How could Jeanette possibly know that I was considering moving to Indiana?"

She continued, "Carl and I have been talking, and we feel God wants you here in Indiana, so we both want you to know that when you're ready to move out here, there's a place for you. You can stay with us."

Well, that solved two obstacles at once. Because I could use the Strohm's home as my legal residence, I would be able to get a phone number *and* a post office box.

I gave God three days to take care of my obstacles, and he handled them in two! In spite of my best efforts, I could not think of a single excuse not to move.

On August 19 at the end of my summer tour in Indianapolis, I flew back to Vancouver to fulfill almost three months of engagements that were waiting for me there. Then on November 10, after my last concert in Vancouver, I got into my little 1984 Nissan Sentra and drove more than 2,000 miles to Indianapolis.

I arrived at the Strohm household at 11:40 p.m. on Thursday, November 13, 1997. That day was one of the happiest, and most terrifying, days of my life.

David Michael Carrillo

Help me not to lean on my mind
Help me to leave the fears behind
Let me see through childlike eyes
That you're with me

From the song *Trust In You*
(David Michael Carrillo © 1989 The Songs of GentleWind)

CHAPTER 8
Learning To Trust

As for God, his way is perfect;
the word of the Lord is flawless.
He is a shield for all who take refuge in him.
Psalm 18:30

*I*n spite of all the good things that happened to me in the time leading up to and immediately following my move to Indianapolis, I never let myself forget how easily a door could slam shut. Although most people could not see it, I continued to harbor a deep-rooted pessimism that forced me always to keep my guard up.

I approached each day hesitantly, waiting for the next major rejection that would rock my world. My music ministry was flourishing, but not my trust in God.

In Matthew 6, Jesus tells his disciples not to worry needlessly about what to eat or to drink or how to clothe their bodies. The birds in the sky and the lilies in the field don't worry about these things, Jesus tells them, and God provides for their every need. The moral of the story, of course, is that if God provides for the lowliest of earth's creatures, then you must trust how much more He will provide for those He created in His own image. God will provide for us no matter what burdens the world puts upon us.

I had heard this passage of scripture many times, but never really embraced or reflected upon its message in my own life. Nevertheless, God, true to His word, fed me spiritually in the way I needed most, at the time I needed it most.

* * * * *

After I moved to Indiana I saw very little of my friend, John Conrad. He had put tremendous effort into establishing a new church on the north side of Indianapolis. Upon accomplishing this and turning the church over to another pastor's capable hands, John accepted a pastoral internship at a Lutheran church near Littleton, Colorado. He was on the road again, and I said goodbye once more to my friend.

In April 1999 John called me to tell me that things were working out well for him in Colorado. He had just returned from a long bike ride with one of his parishioners, and they had been discussing the more difficult aspects of being a pastor. "Dealing with the tragic deaths," John said to me. "You know, David Michael, I'm always shaken by the tragic deaths."

I knew what he meant. I remembered my own experience in Derby Acres trying to minister to the parents of the infant who had drowned in a swimming pool. There was no clear way to minister to a grieving family suffering from the trauma of a tragic death.

Ironically, one day after this conversation, on April 20th, John and I joined the rest of the country in shock and grief over the tragic loss of 13 souls, 12 students and 1 teacher, at the hands of two teenage boys who went on a shooting rampage and then committed suicide at Columbine High School in Littleton, Colorado.

When the shootings started John and the head pastor of his church, along with the pastors of several nearby churches, were called to the site to help minister to the families who were waiting for news about their children. The students, as you might recall, were held hostage for several hours, and many parents spent those hours in agony wondering if their sons or daughters were among those injured, killed, or still held captive inside the school.

John was assigned to minister to the family of Corey DePooter. Sadly, Corey was among the students who were killed in the school library. When the DePooter's finally learned of their son's fate, they turned to John and asked him if he would do their son's service. John called me and asked for my prayers, which, of course, I gave freely. In the days that followed, I watched the news about Columbine unfold on television, and wished I could do more.

John called me again later in the week to let me know that he had given Mrs. DePooter one of my CDs. He told me that he prayed it would minister to her, and he asked me to pray for that as well.

The following Monday, nearly one week after the tragedy, I stood in the kitchen washing dishes. I watched the soapy water swirl over the plates, and suddenly, an image came to my mind. I was standing before a sea of faces, dressed in my black shirt and holding my guitar. A woman came up to me and hugged me. It was a big, warm hug. I couldn't see her face, but I felt strongly connected to her. The image faded as the phone rang; it was John.

"David Michael, I've bought you a ticket and I need you to get on a plane within the hour."

"What do you mean?" I said.

"You're going to sing at the funeral of Corey DePooter."

"What do you mean?" I asked again.

"Mrs. DePooter came to my office today," John explained. "She told me that after I handed her your recording and left, she put on the tape. She said the first verse of the first song brought her such peace that she fell right asleep. She hadn't slept in four days. Since then she has played the recording over and over again. When I saw her today, she asked me if we could play your tape at her son's funeral because she felt so comforted by it."

"I hope you'll forgive me," John said, "but I told her I wasn't going to play the tape – because I would bring you here in person instead. So, David Michael, you have to catch a plane right away."

A friend helped me pack and drove me to the airport. When I arrived in Littleton, the message boards all over the highways read, "Colorado grieves together." The flashing letters illuminated a message of unity, a message of hope. "God help me," I prayed. "Help me to be a messenger of hope."

The next day was Tuesday, April 27, one week after the shootings. At 11:20 a.m., the church bells in Littleton rang to mark the one-week anniversary of the deaths of the 13 souls at Columbine. Later that day I entered Trinity Christian Center, the church where most of the funerals were conducted. John arrived soon after, and we went off together for a moment to pray. Then John introduced me to the DePooter's.

Mrs. DePooter walked up to me, arms wide open, and gave me a huge hug. "You have a friend for life," she said. "Thank you so much for being here." Her warmth was so moving in the midst of the overwhelming heartbreak that surrounded us.

I was ushered to the front of the church with all the guest speakers, and waited somberly, and somewhat uneasily, as the friends and family of Corey DePooter arrived. I don't think anyone can be prepared to attend the funeral of a young person, especially when you realize this is funeral number five in a string of funerals. For the fifth day in a row the same people had returned to the same church to say goodbye to another student.

I looked at their faces, so many young faces. They said everything and nothing at the same time. The tragedy had wiped away every pretension. The expressions of grief ranged from frightened stares, to gut-wrenching cries, to quiet sighs of exhaustion.

What can I possibly say, I thought, after five funerals that will make any difference? I was on the schedule to sing "Trust in You," a song I wrote nearly ten years ago during my ministry in Derby Acres. When it was my turn to address the congregation, I approached the stage anxiously and sang the words as if for the first time.

> *When fear is like a raging river*
> *And the hope I built is on sinking sand*
> *Help me build my faith, Lord, on dry land*
> *Upon the rock of salvation I shall stand*
>
> *Help me not to lean on my mind*
> *Help me to leave the fears behind*
> *Let me see through childlike eyes*
> *That you're with me*
> *Through the darkest times of my life*

I looked out among the sea of faces, strumming my guitar, dressed in my black shirt, and suddenly I realized I had seen all of this before. This was the image I had seen while washing dishes in my kitchen just one day before. Now, I promise I'm no prophet, but I do believe that God tries to prepare you from time to time for the work he desires to accomplish, and at that moment I felt assured that I was where I needed to be.

To this day I still struggle to understand what happened in Littleton, Colorado, on April 20, 1999. The tragedy at Columbine High School revealed the evil in men's hearts, but that was not its defining message. For those who died, for those who gathered to grieve, and for those who assembled to comfort the grief-stricken, God was there. Through a multitude of instruments of grace, God ministered to the hearts of those who placed their trust in him. I saw it on the flashing highway message boards, I heard it in the ringing of the church bells, I felt it in Mrs. DePooter's hug and in the prayers of the faithful. God was there.

* * * * *

The events in Littleton touched me deeply. Never before had I played a role in such an immense tragedy outside of my own small circle of personal experience. For the first time, I began to contemplate the supremacy of the Lord's presence in each and every human life.

In May of 1999 I set off on another series of concerts for a community of Lutheran churches. Less than one month after the Columbine tragedy, my heart was still heavy with sorrow. I attended Sunday service at the Lutheran church that hosted my tour, and went to receive communion. The pastor handed me the bread, looked at me, and said, "Body of Christ."

Body of Christ. I had heard these words before, but now they startled me. *Body of Christ.* As the pastor said this, I heard in my heart, "This is my body, David Michael, that was beaten, whipped, pierced, and nailed to a cross for you because I love you." *Blood of Christ.* "And this blood, David Michael, I poured out. I shed freely to wash away your sins, to give you hope and a future because I love you."

I was standing at the front of the church holding the bread and wine, and the truth of that moment suddenly swept over me. Everyone who went up to receive communion that day was standing before God, broken and bruised by their own stories of suffering. I was no different. My suffering was no different. Growing up I might have been beaten by my classmates, ridiculed and discarded by my peers, but Jesus never rejected me. *Jesus never rejected me.*

I continued to stare at the bread and wine, the substance of our communion with the body and blood of Christ, and I realized "You did this for me! You love me that much. I do have hope. I do have a future."

Tears poured from my eyes. My perspective changed instantly. I had always known I was loved by God, but until that moment I had never trusted that He accepted me as one of His own, as a member of the body of Christ. Now, I understood the awesome depth of His love.

* * * * *

One week after this startling revelation I met Anthony Todd Ping. I believe that by bringing Todd into my life at that time, God was finding another instrument of grace to provide for me spiritually at a critical point in the evolution of my ministry. Today I count Todd as one of my best friends and spiritual mentors, but forging that friendship was a rocky road.

Todd is one of those guys who doesn't let you get away with anything – the kind you can count on to be brutally honest and to push you outside of your comfort zone, kicking and screaming if necessary. I think the Lord knew that he was exactly the kind of friend I needed at that point in my life.

My ministry was successful, but my performances had become routine. I knew the Lord was using each of my concerts, but I also knew I wasn't making the most of my gifts. I had grown accustomed to living and performing within my comfort zone.

After watching several of my performances, Todd spotted this and offered some constructive criticism. "This ministry is not about you, David Michael; it's about the Lord. It's about walking in the spirit and connecting with the hearts of the people."

Where had I heard that before? The words of the young pastor from the little white church in Derby Acres surfaced again.

In August 1999 Todd became a full partner in my ministry. For five years he handled the business side of the ministry: booking tours, launching a Web site, and handling expenses. Most importantly, he challenged me to get out of my shell and to start writing music that came from personal experience.

It was Todd who helped me to deal with my ADHD and to translate my personal struggles into music that ministers to the souls of others coping with the same challenges. That wasn't easy for me, or for him. After being my roommate for two years on a particularly intensive schedule of back-to-back concerts, Todd endured firsthand the roller coaster ride of my feelings of inferiority, lack of focus, and overreactions.

"C'mon," he barked one day. "This is totally inappropriate. You're overreacting. This isn't how a minister should act." I can't remember what I did to set him off, but I know his reaction was probably more appropriate than mine.

Todd was like a coach to me. He encouraged me to train myself to think things through first and speak later. He'd say,

"Ok, stop. Let's take a breath and try it from here." I didn't like his criticism, but now I realize that he saw something I just didn't see at the time. He helped me to stretch myself as a minister and as a songwriter.

I never thought I would be able to talk to an audience about my ADHD and other disabilities, or to share my testimony, but with Todd's help, I did. I never thought I would be able to write songs about those experiences, but thanks to Todd, I did. *Fearfully and Wonderfully Made, Wounds of Pain, He Flew Away, Dusty Road, Caught in the Middle* – all of these songs were born out of my personal struggles, and they represent a genre of music I had never tried before.

* * * * *

Ironically, the aspects of my life that I believed were not worth sharing, that I spent years trying to hide, were the very things that people wanted most to hear about. My praise and worship ministry turned into a sort of praise-worship-preaching-singing-workshop ministry. To this day, the parents of children with ADHD who attend my workshops are amazed to see on the stage a relatively composed person with ADHD playing a classical guitar.

Some of them come up to me in tears afterwards and hug me. Through my experience, they tell me, they see hope for their own children. I often hear, "You gave us hope," or "You gave us information about ADHD we never had before," or "You helped us to finally understand our child."

I am truly humbled by people's reactions to my concerts and workshops. Whenever I begin to doubt what I'm doing – and yes, I confess, I'm still inclined to do that, especially when bookings slow down and the stacks of bills increase – I remember the words of a thankful parent, the letter of a teacher, or the hug of a child who is struggling like I once did (and still do).

My music ministry might not be as vast or as popular as that of the Michael W. Smith's of the Christian music industry, but that's okay. With God's grace I'm reaching a special group of people who might not otherwise be reached.

God has blessed me with unique gifts for a unique ministry that I hope with all my heart is helping people with ADHD and other learning disabilities learn how to turn their personal stumbling blocks into stepping stones.

* * * * *

It's been a difficult journey. Once I realized that the Lord, and the Lord alone, never rejected me, I learned to place my trust in Him and His people. As a member of the body of Christ, I have started to understand the discipline and obedience necessary to seek and follow His will, not mine – and to become truly an instrument of His grace.

I first sensed this spiritual truth during the funeral service for Corey DePooter, although I wasn't confident then that I fully understood it or knew how to respond to it. Todd, however, saw the potential in me. At times, he probably felt like he had to beat it out of me. Todd helped take my ministry to the next level, which opened doors that led to a new album, to the ADHD workshop, and even to a new book.

Todd remains a good friend, although sadly for me I had to say goodbye to him in 2004 when he moved to Alaska to start a new ministry to bring more hearts to the Lord. Today I share my music and workshop ministry with another good friend, Ryan Zachariah Noll, who coincidentally also struggles with ADHD. Zachariah is a talented musician and inspirational speaker. For several years, however, he chose a life of gangs and drugs as an antidote to the constant rejections and failed relationships he experienced in his youth. When Zachariah found love and forgiveness in the Lord, he was able to break the bonds of addiction that trapped him. With the Lord's help he continues to grow spiritually day by day. He is a devoted father to four beautiful children, and he eagerly seeks opportunities to speak to youth groups about the dangers of drug abuse and gang life.

Through amazing events and through amazing people, I have discovered that learning to trust in the Lord is a great spiritual odyssey. It is not smooth sailing by any means. The devil seeks every opportunity to throw you off course. But only when you allow the Lord to steer, it is then that you begin to find your way.

I've seen your hand in my life
In all you've brought me through
Lord, you've been so faithful and true

From the song *Faithful*
(David Michael Carrillo © 1990/2005 The Songs of GentleWind)

David Michael Carrillo

CHAPTER 9
Fearfully and Wonderfully Made

*I praise you because I am fearfully and wonderfully made;
your works are wonderful...*
Psalm 139:14

When I was a little boy, my mother liked to remind me that even before I was "knit in her womb," God knew me. I wasn't a mistake. I wasn't forgotten. I was "fearfully and wonderfully made" in God's image. He had a plan for me.

Back then I found it hard to appreciate those words, or to admit that my mother was right. When I wrote the song *Fearfully and Wonderfully Made*, it was in part to honor my mother's faithful efforts to help me discover the true meaning of King David's inspired words in Psalm 139.

What does it mean to be fearfully and wonderfully made?

When we are fearful of God, we are obedient to His authority. We accept that He is the Lord of hosts, the King of glory, our one true Master, and we serve Him alone. He is the Good Shepherd, and we are His sheep. As Psalm 23 tells us, when we follow Him, we shall be led along the right paths, and He shall restore our soul.

We are wonderfully made because we are made in God's image. When we accept this as truth, how can we go wrong? No matter what trials life throws our way, we cannot fail if God is in us, and we are in Him. God is our true life coach, and our greatest cheerleader. We will succeed if we trust Him and freely use the gifts of grace that He gives generously to each and every one of us.

David Michael Carrillo

* * * * *

I have learned the hard way that to curse my life is, in a sense, to curse God. He sent His only son, Jesus Christ, to suffer and die for me, for all of us, so that through this greatest sacrifice you and I may live to share in the eternal kingdom of God.

In Romans 8:17, the apostle Paul tells us that as children of God, we are the "heirs" of the kingdom as well, "co-heirs with Christ," but *only* if "we share in his sufferings in order that we may also share in his glory."

We live in an imperfect world ravaged by crises and tragedies of every kind; there is no question that we all must suffer. In fact, the question is not if, but when. And when our time comes to suffer, how will we cope with our afflictions in light of the suffering Christ endured for all mankind?

The day I throw in the towel and declare that my own suffering is too great, that my ADHD and the problems it causes in my life are more than I can bear, that is the day I choose not to suffer *with* Christ, but apart from Him. That would be a sad day indeed because suffering apart from Christ starts us on that downward spiral of self pity, that leads to despair, that leads to hopelessness. It suctions us into the black hole of selfishness that blinds us to God's "wonderful works" within ourselves and within others.

* * * * *

Many people who have ADHD and other learning disabilities can suffer greatly. They might suffer physically, but to a greater extent, they suffer emotionally. Society puts labels on them. Friends and family lose patience and struggle to maintain relationships with them. Doctors can be too quick to treat them as guinea pigs to test and promote the latest drug therapies.

These days it is too easy to focus on the problems of ADHD rather than to see the wonders of God's works within the children and adults who have this condition.

Like all of God's children, people with ADHD have amazing gifts. More often than not, these gifts include being exceptionally creative and energetic, and able to perceive the most astonishing levels of detail in one's surroundings. People with ADHD *experience more* of their environment than others do.

Personally, I feel as if I observe the world in full color with a panoramic view, while others may see it more narrowly in black and white. The main challenge for people who have ADHD is that we have such a heightened sensitivity to every detail of our environment that we find it difficult to focus on any one thing.

On the other hand, because we see and hear so much of the world, we can offer more interesting insights, more original perspectives. So, for persons like me with ADHD, the challenge is to find ways to tame the wild streaks of this condition so that we can discover and use the unique spiritual gifts that God has given us.

A good analogy I like to use is the kaleidoscope. Kaleidoscopes contain hundreds, sometimes thousands, of pieces of multi-colored fragments. Left alone, these pieces form nothing more than a pile of colorful clutter. But when pointed toward the light and shifted carefully with a slight turn of hand, the colorful fragments come together in vibrant patterns to create beautiful, luminous images.

David Michael Carrillo

This is the image I had in mind when I started my "Living a Colorful Life" ADHD workshop ministry. *Living a colorful life* is my way of patterning my ADHD, and the gifts it brings with it, so that the wonderful works of God can be made manifest. If you recall the story of the blind man in John 9, which I use to open this book, there is nothing in this world that cannot be used to reveal the goodness of God's glory.

*****

It has taken me a long time to accept that God has given me a unique way of seeing the world – and, most importantly, to accept that this is a good thing. I hated so much about myself growing up: my bony fingers, my high-pitched voice, my goofy boundless energy. But those fingers strum my guitar, the voice expresses my songs, and the energy helps me to travel to distant places and to relate to so many people. The very things I counted as "mistakes" in my life are actually the gifts God gave me as a means to share in his glory.

We are all fearfully and wonderfully made to love and to serve God. You and I are not mistakes! Each of us has a distinct purpose in God's kingdom. The truest joy in life is to discover what that purpose is – to embark on the adventure of faith – and then to live in accordance with God's will, fruitfully and abundantly.

For those of you with ADHD, and for those of you who love someone with ADHD, I pray that you will commit each day to living a colorful life, to finding hope in the hardship, and to trusting in God's providence and all His wondrous works. Peace is found only in Him.

Fearfully and Wonderfully Made

Before you were born
God knew your name
Your life is not a mistake
You are fearfully and wonderfully made

From the song *Fearfully and Wonderfully Made*
(David Michael Carrillo © 2002 The Songs of GentleWind)

David Michael Carrillo

CHAPTER 10
Living a Colorful Life

May your deeds be shown to your servants,
your splendor to their children.
Psalm 90:16

This chapter is for anyone with ADHD, but especially for those who live or work with someone with ADHD. In my workshops I good-naturedly call the latter group the "black-and-white world," in other words, those people who can reliably abide by social norms and find it difficult, therefore, to see life through the colorful, chaotic, 3D lens of ADHD.

As Christians we have to be very careful about overlooking – or worse yet, discounting – those members of the body of Christ who might be outside the boundaries of the "black-and-white world." As a child I encountered many Christians who were quick to scold, ignore, or lose patience with me, but very few who took the time to seek the gifts of Christ within me. Those who did, however, made a positive and indelible impression on me and the course of my life.

Why is it so easy to hear the Word of God, and so hard to live it? For Christians, the Word of God can be truly stimulating. It can inspire awesome sermons, lively debates, and stirring forms of prayer and worship. All of these are good things. But if we're not careful, we can reduce Scripture to a sort of aphrodisiac, drinking it in only to satisfy our creature comforts or intellectual curiosities, and offering nothing of substance to the kingdom of God in return.

We are told in the first chapter of James to be doers and not just receivers of the Word. In James 2:14-17, it is written

"What good is it, my brothers, if a man claims to have faith but has no deeds? Can such faith save him? Suppose a brother or sister is without clothes and daily food. If one of you says to him, 'Go, I wish you well; keep warm and well fed,' but does nothing about his physical needs, what good is it? In the same way, faith by itself, if it is not accompanied by action, is dead."

We all need to practice at inviting God's Word to *live* in our hearts. For those of us with ADHD, that means first and foremost believing we're NOT mistakes. God in his infinite wisdom designed all of humanity with a purpose in mind. We must use God's word as a "shield of armor" to endure and overcome the battles of life with ADHD so that we can discover and then use the gifts He gave us to reveal His divine purpose.

For those who live and work with someone with ADHD, that means having patience and realizing that people with ADHD or other learning disabilities need to encounter your gifts of faith and acts of Christian love. Don't be afraid. Don't lose hope. The secret weapons are faith, hope, and love. With these three, you can help manage the colorful life of ADHD in a positive, purposeful way.

Here are some ways that parents (and significant others) can help children with ADHD embark on their own spiritual journey to live a colorful life according to God's divine purpose. Although these, of course, can apply for all children, they are especially beneficial for children with ADHD.

Pray with your child every day

Watching and hearing my mother pray started me on my Christian faith journey that eventually led to my music and workshop ministry. Daily prayer is essential for all of us, although for the ADHD child, learning how to be still and to pray in the traditional sense can seem like an impossible task. As a result, you may need to find a way to make prayer appealing in a colorful way for the ADHD child. For me, hearing my mother pray *in song* captured my attention more vividly than traditional, meditative prayer would have. Other options might be to read pop-up books that illustrate "The Lord's Prayer" or to put up colorful wall hangings of select verses from the "Book of Psalms" or to make mobiles of well-known bible scenes such as The Nativity or The Lord's Supper. There are also creative ways to engage your child in the daily rituals of saying grace before meals and bedtime prayers. Praying for and with your ADHD child every day will help them to nurture the most important relationship they will ever know (especially on those days when it might seem like all other relationships fail them).

Give hugs and lots of them!

ADHD kids thrive on affection and encouragement. In fact, they need more of it than most children because they get so easily frustrated and anxious. Nothing was more meaningful to me as a child than to get a great big hug from my mom or dad. On the other hand, nothing was more painful, physically and emotionally, than to get a slap on the backside, speaking of which....

Use spanking prudently as a form of discipline

Children with ADHD are capable of learning right from wrong; in fact, most are quick to point out other children who are "being bad." But they lack the "on/off switch" that tells them to mentally stop and consider the consequences of an action before they take it. As a result, you can easily find a reason to spank or yell at an ADHD child every hour of every day, but that won't help them learn how to manipulate that mental on/off switch. Excessive or reactive spankings and angry verbal rebukes, however, will spiritually demoralize the ADHD child very easily. As I child, I remembered sharply the spankings I received from my mother, but I rarely understood the behaviors on my part that led up to them. That mental disconnect resulted in more hardship than was necessary, for both my mother and for me. There are many good resources on how to help ADHD children manage their hyperactive, inattentive, or impulsive behaviors. Take time to study these and learn the approaches that work best for your child.

Teach your child to take breaks in order to be more productive

ADHD children rarely perceive when they need to slow down and take a break. They can be like wind-up toys that never stop until they hit the wall. The end result for them can be to experience only the feelings of frustration that come with living in a state of perpetual motion yet achieving nothing productive. I've found that when I'm working for a long time on a new song or trying to get through the bills, I need to allow myself short breaks by taking a walk or spending time with my cats; otherwise, I can't concentrate. By taking a series of short breaks throughout a task, I can actually complete the task. Of course, I have to be careful about not using my break time as a launching pad for a new task. To prevent this, I schedule my time very carefully. Mondays are for paying bills, Tuesdays and Wednesdays are for rehearsing, Thursdays are for administrative tasks like replying to emails and updating my Web site, and Fridays are usually rest and relaxation days since I do most of my concerts and workshops over the weekend.

Most importantly, this schedule is written down; it's visible and tangible, not just a mental to-do list. Without this kind of visually-reinforced regimen I will inevitably get lost in the sea of daily responsibilities. Today, you can teach ADHD children how to plan their tasks (and break times) with the help of all kinds of visual aids and gadgets, from dry-erase boards to magnetic wall charts to computer desktop calendars to palm pilots. Of course, a church calendar or an old-fashioned spiral notepad and pen can work just as well.

Build a network of supportive family and friends

It can be difficult to interact with an ADHD child. Don't expect neighbors, teachers, friends, and family to know instinctively how to relate to your child. Do make an effort, however, to seek out those people who might be the most supportive and nurturing with your child, educate them about ADHD as appropriate, and encourage their participation in your child's life. I recall, for example, that there wasn't much I enjoyed about school. In fact, I tore up just about every class picture of myself from the age of 8 to 18. But I do remember those few extraordinary teachers who refused to label me as a discipline problem and who made the effort to encourage my musical gifts. Without their kindness and patience I might have given in to total despair. The summer camp counselor who lets you (safely) make big splashes in the pool, the Sunday school teacher who lets you "act out" a bible story while she narrates it, the uncle who happily chases you around the yard at family cookouts – all of these are spiritual gems to the ADHD child, who more often than not has a tendency to feel disconnected with the rest of the world.

Help your child discover his or her spiritual gifts through play

Children with ADHD have one particularly fascinating trait. Most of the time, they can feel overwhelmed to the point of paralysis by all of the competing stimuli in their environment – until something breaks through and captures their attention. And from that moment on, that one "thing," whatever it is, will receive their complete, undivided focus and mental energy. This is not always a good thing. For example, for very young children with ADHD, the object of their attention might be an open car door or a boiling pot of water on a stove. Clearly in these cases, you need to immediately redirect their attention, and at times their physical presence, for their own safety. But when you see this phenomenon occur during play periods, be alert. Many spiritual gifts are discovered through intense, concentrated play, and this is especially true for the ADHD child. My favorite play activities as a young child were listening to music on headphones, listening to (and watching) records on spinning turntables, and making my puppets sing and perform skits during "The Learning Show." Music and performing were clearly my "thing," and in time they were nurtured to reveal a true spiritual gift. Give your child lots of opportunities for safe and constructive play, and observe them carefully. During those moments, spiritual gifts may emerge that will serve them (and God's will) for a lifetime.

Involve your child in charitable activities

ADHD kids love to please and can express great concern for people in need. Find opportunities to nurture this instinct by involving your child in acts of charity, such as grocery shopping for canned food drives, buying a Christmas present for a needy child, or helping to wash grandpa's car. Of course, you'll want to find those tasks that allow them to be creative and at times even messy. Encouraging these acts of kindness not only bolsters their feelings of self worth, but also helps ADHD children to look beyond their own wants and desires in order to *see* the needs of others in very real, compelling ways. And in the process, you may also do a great service to those members of the "black-and-white world" who can learn a lot about *how* to give from the ADHD child, who often gives so generously and so cheerfully. God loves a cheerful giver!

Living a colorful life in a "black-and-white world" is more of a philosophy than a formula for managing ADHD. There will be ups and downs, frustrations and failures – a lot of them. But the Lord who loves you will provide for you. Trust in Him, and your spiritual life will shine brilliantly!

Fearfully and Wonderfully Made
(David Michael Carrillo © 2002 The Songs of GentleWind)

She got the news that her son
Would not be like everyone
He would have challenges
And four little letters will define him

He's forced to stand on the playground
The other kids don't want him around
Mama, why was I born
To live a life of shame and scorn?

And his mother's heart would break
Over the comments that he'd make
So she held her son in her arms
And she would whisper in his ear
So that he could clearly hear
What God above sees in her son

Before you were born
God knew your name
Your life is not a mistake
You are fearfully and wonderfully made

Before you were born
God knew your name
Your life is not a mistake
In his image you are made

Before you were born
God called your name
Your life is not a mistake
You are fearfully and wonderfully made